Be Not Afraid

Charles Tom —
all my Best

Peter Dent

3/8/04

Be Not Afraid
Ben Peyton's Story

A SEVENTEEN-YEAR-OLD HOCKEY
PLAYER'S FIGHT TO OVERCOME A
DEVASTATING INJURY

Peter Rennebohm

NORTH STAR PRESS OF ST. CLOUD, INC.

ISBN: 0-87839-205-X

First edition, March 2004

Printed in the United States by Versa Press, Inc.
East Peoria, Illinois

Published by
North Star Press of St. Cloud, Inc.
P.O. Box 451
St. Cloud, Minnesota 56302
nspress@cloudnet.com

Dedicated to
DALE HOLMES RENNEBOHM
All American—Football
University of Minnesota
1935 National Champions

Who loved watching us play our sports—especially
hockey.

He was my dad and I was proud of him

Acknowledgements

My heartfelt thank you to: My wife, Shari for enduring my somewhat peculiar, late-in-life passion to write. Daughters Jenny and Emily for always believing in me. My very dear friend Tom Carlson, who from the beginning urged me to pursue my dream. Michael O'Rourke, friend and novelist, for his guidance and example. Harvey Stanbrough, poet, mentor, and friend. Corinne Dwyer and North Star Press for giving life and credence to this project. All the friends and relatives of the Peytons—indeed the entire Edina community—for their prayers and constant support of Ben. Joe Schmit, Lou Nanne, Senator Norm Coleman, and Congressman James Ramstad for their kind words. And finally, the Peytons—John, Nancy, Ben and Annie for allowing me to intrude, prod, question and interpret what were very private thoughts and feelings. They opened up their hearts so we all could share in their marvelous, courageous, and inspirational story.

Peter Rennebohm

Foreword

by
Joe Schmit

The Ben Peyton story is a true tragedy-to-triumph story. Ben's courage may have been exceeded only by the incredible outpouring of love from family, friends, and the hockey community in Minnesota and beyond. I vividly recall in one of the darkest moments following the accident, Ben's dad told me, "It might be hard to believe, but this was the best thing that ever happened to this family." Words like "inspiration" are overused today, but the word might not be strong enough when describing Ben Peyton's story. Ben's "be not afraid" attitude had as much to do with his recovery as all the outstanding medical care he received.

I remember producing my first story on Ben, and something strange happened, something that has only happened a couple of times in my career. I had a difficult time writing the script. There were all the elements of a great story, but I felt pressure putting his remarkable story down on paper because I was afraid I could not do it justice. This was not only a story about a young man battling for his life and later for his quality of live, this was a story of how one moment in time touched the heart and soul of literally thousands of people.

Ben was a kid who grew up on skates and grew out of skates, but he will never skate again because of the injury he sustained. In his wheelchair, Ben told me that he had vivid dreams about walking again. His dream came true one small victory at a time. Ben Peyton is living proof that a body might break down, but that alone can't break down the human spirit, especially one with an iron will.

Joe Schmit
KSTP-TV
Sports Director

Table of Contents

Ben Peyton—center—Edina Gold, November 1996.

Chapter One

A Parent's Worst Nightmare

ECEMBER 22, 1996—THE WINTER SOLSTICE. For the Peyton family, the shortest day of the year became the longest of their lives. That was the day when everything changed forever.

The Minnetonka Ice Arena was filled to capactiy. Parents, friends, and students cheered, blew loud horns, stamped their feet and clapped gloved hands. Sharpened blades dug into the smooth ice. Each pair of skates carved erratic arcs and deep, linear grooves. The sounds of metal on ice combined with the *slap-slap* of stick on stick, stick on frozen rubber, and filled the small arena.

1

The Edina Junior Gold team had just been whistled for icing—the face-off would be deep in their zone. Seventeen-year-old Ben Peyton glided to the face-off circle and leaned over, anticipating the drop of the puck.

The referee quickly dropped the puck. Ben and the opposing center scrambled for control of the black disc. Another Edina player raced in and jabbed the puck loose. He gained control and skated behind the net. Ben wheeled out of the offensive zone, glanced back at his teammate with the puck and skated hard toward his own blue line. Just as he cleared the zone, the defenseman sent the puck in Ben's direction. The green-and-gold-clad youngster took one quick look at the opposing defenseman and readied to receive the pass.

John and Nancy Peyton stood along the boards in the Edina end of the rink. Just as they had done hundreds of times before, they stood watching their son play hockey.

"No! Don't make that pass. Dump it in," John said, speaking of the Edina defenseman. *It's a sucker pass.* "Get your head up, Ben." John feared what was about to happen. He pressed both hands against the Plexiglas surrounding the rink and watched helplessly.

Nancy glanced at her husband briefly and turned back to the action on the ice.

Like watching a video at slow speed, John and Nancy watched Ben and an opposing player skate toward each other. Their crash was inevitable, and all

2

the two parents could do was watch and hope. There was nothing they could do to stop the action on the ice.

Ben was seventeen, a junior at Edina High School, playing center for the Edina Junior Gold hockey team. A developmental league, the team comprised well-conditioned boys honing their skills to play on the varsity team the following year.

Ben wheeled out of his defensive zone, glanced left and saw one of his defensemen with the puck. He skated hard across his blue line. Just as he reached center ice, this teammate fed him the puck. Ben took one quick look at the opposing defenseman closing in on him, then readied himself for the pass.

His neck was sore and stiff from the previous day, and he didn't have full range of motion in it. Ben's team was playing in a holiday tournament. The evening before, in a semifinal game, an opposing player whacked him across the neck with his stick.

Teammates and friends thought that was particularly vicious, and Ben felt pain and stiffness all night. By Sunday morning, the day of the championship game, he could barely turn his head. He briefly considered not skating that day, but, by game time, his neck had loosened enough that he decided to play.

As he tried to look to his left for the puck, he felt awkward and restricted. From the corner of his eye, he saw the puck leave the defenseman's stick, but he also realized that he was going too fast. The puck would strike his skates, not his stick.

He sensed the opposing defenseman closing in as the puck reached his skate blade. He looked down and moved to kick the disc forward to his stick just as the other player hit him. With both elbows up, the opposing player hit Ben high and hard.

Ben's parents watched him attempt to receive the puck. John knew what would happen next. The hard, black disc was slow and late in arriving. Ben took the pass in his skates, then, just as he kicked it forward, he collided with the other player.

Hockey players are permitted to check their opponents as long as they either have possession of the puck or were the last player to touch it. The player is permitted two strides only before making contact with his opponent.

The defenseman who hit Ben that Sunday took more than the two allowed steps and then hit Ben with his elbows up, moving at full stride. The sound of the collision was audible throughout the arena. They hit with a tremendous thud, a sickening sound. Ben's parents heard it and felt the impact as the two young bodies struck.

Ben saw it coming but had no time to brace himself. His head snapped back viciously, and his feet left the ice as he was propelled up and back. Landing on the back of his neck, he lay motionless, his arms and legs splayed to the sides. Strangely, there was no pain—or any other feeling.

John and Nancy had seen Ben hit that hard before. The impacts often looked worse than the one they just witnessed, and Ben had always gotten up

John waits for Ben to get up.

and skated off afterwards.

Come on, Ben, John begged. *Get up!*

John couldn't move, his eyes riveted to his son on the ice. Like a petrified tree, he stood leaning against the glass, his fingers as white as ice, the color drained from his face. He watched in horror as the referee signaled a time out and motioned for help.

Ben's coach ran onto the ice and slid to a stop beside Ben. Players from both teams gathered around.

When Nancy saw her son hit the ice, she knew he was in trouble. She ran down the sideboards toward the players' box, shouting, "John! You'd better come!"

John, still caught in the nightmare of the moment, didn't want to move, though he knew he must. He was paralyzed by the thought of dealing with the horrific possibilities of what had happened to his son on the ice. *If I stand here just a little longer, Ben will move, and the nightmare will end. Please, let it end!*

It didn't. Ben wasn't moving. Suddenly, everything speeded up, and John ran out to join his wife and son on the ice.

Two of Ben's teammates escorted Nancy from the players' box to where Ben lay.

"Ben?" This was all she could say when she reached him.

"I'm sorry, Mom," Ben said calmly. "I can't feel my arms or legs."

Dropping to her knees, she placed her hands on either side of Ben's face. She forced her concerns from her face. She had to be calm and strong. If she burst into tears, Ben would be frightened. She looked down and saw fear in his eyes. He lay spread-eagled, like an immobile snow angel.

"The paramedics are on their way, Mrs. Peyton," the coach said. "They'll be here in a few minutes."

The coach and other concerned people—other players' parents—blocked Ben's head on either side to stabilize him until the medics arrived. His vision was then limited to what he could see directly overhead.

He looked at the large scoreboard with the clock on it. The score was three to three, with nine minutes left in the game. The clock read 1:30. Ben squinted at the bright light and moved his eyes slowly to the left, toward his mother.

Nancy followed each movement of her son's eyes, the only part of him that moved. She saw fear first and wished she could erase the last few seconds of play. She wanted to crawl inside Ben to share what he thought and felt.

Following his gaze upward, Nancy saw the clock, wondering why he stared so intently at the time. She shook her head and looked back down at Ben.

He glanced beyond this mother and saw his father for the first time, standing behind her. John looked ready to throw up. His face was white, like the ice on which Ben sprawled. "Dad," he said, "are you okay?"

Too sick to reply, John looked down at his son and thought, *He's concerned about me! Leave it to Ben.* Bile rose in his throat and settled on the back of his tongue. His eyes filled with tears as he looked at his son. *I'm ready to puke,* he thought. *What's wrong with me?*

Kneeling beside Nancy, John put his hand over hers, took a deep breath and looked into Ben's eyes. "I'm okay, Ben. Try not to talk."

As Ben lay on the ice with his worried parents overhead, he felt his condition was only temporary. Soon, he'd regain some feeling, like the football player with the Cincinnati Bengals. *What is his name? Scott Blumfeld. He was able to get up and walk again after thirty minutes.*

"Dad, where are my arms right now?" Ben asked. "They're up over my head, right?"

John stared and hesitated before saying, "No, Ben. They're down at your side."

The family had discussed the possibility of

injuries beforehand. John knew that one of his son's biggest fears was having to go into the corners of the rink after a puck, knowing that an opposing player could run him into the boards.

"It didn't happen in the corner, did it, Dad?" Ben asked, slowly beginning to realize the seriousness of his injury. "It happened in the middle of the ice."

Ben started to become truly scared. The fearful looks on the faces around him had unsettled him.

John and Nancy Peyton wait for the paramedics.

Whenever Ben was upset, frightened or distraught, he talked a lot. That tendency didn't change on the ice that day.

"Mom? Remember to call my teachers, okay? Looks like I'll miss a few days of school. Dad, get my hockey stick, okay? When's Annie's game? Wait until her game's over before you call her. Dad, what about my car? Will you get someone to drive it home for me?"

Ben kept talking as the paramedics hustled onto the ice. They took over, sliding Ben onto a board to stabilize his head and neck. Then they picked up the litter and set it on a gurney already waiting. As they wheeled Ben from the arena, his parents accompanied him, walking on either side of the gurney.

The longest day in the Peytons' lives was just beginning.

WHILE BEN PLAYED HIS GAME at the Minnetonka Arena, Annie Peyton skated with the boys' Pee-Wee-B team at Braemar Arena in Edina. John and Nancy had decided to watch Ben's game that day. Annie was driven to her game by a friend, Casey Hankinson.

After much family discussion and a lot of trepidation, the Peytons had decided to allow Annie to play in the rougher boys' league that year. For the first time, the Pee-Wee boys' hockey leagues were allowed to body check. Annie was thirteen, an extremely good hockey player; she had no trouble playing with the larger boys despite her small stature. She loved the game, and her parents knew it.

After Annie's game ended, Casey came to the locker room to pick her up. By then, word of Ben's injury had already spread. "Annie, Ben's been injured." His expression indicated it was serious.

"Huh? How? What happened?" Assuming he'd broken a leg, she waited for Casey's response.

"I don't know the details. I'm supposed to take you back to your house. Your mom will call later." Casey refused to elaborate although he knew more.

"We were going out to dinner tonight to celebrate my adoption," Annie said.

"Was this the anniversary of the day your mother brought you home from Bogota?"

"Yes. Thirteen years ago. We'll have to do it another time," she said sadly, unaware that her remembrance would be postponed indefinitely.

BEN CONTINUED CHATTING WITH the paramedics enroute to the ambulance, still hoping his injury was temporary. Conversation was an intentional diversion from his condition. "Hey! About time you guys got here. Where you taking me, anyway?"

"Methodist Hospital," one of the EMTs said.

"You guys play hockey?"

"I was never much of a skater," one of them said. "Jim, you played, didn't you?"

"Yeah, but that was years ago," his partner said.

"Ever get checked so hard you couldn't feel anything?"

The two paramedics looked at each other, reluctant to answer.

"Guess not," Ben said. He turned his eyes to his mother. "Mom, are you coming with me?"

"Yes. I'll be in the front seat, Sweetheart."

"What about you, Dad?"

"Huh? I'll take the car, Benny." John's sense of helplessness was totally debilitating. "I'll follow you to the hospital."

Ben's question surprised him. John hadn't begun to think about how he'd get to the hospital. He shook his head, trying to clear his mind. *Get a grip, for crying out loud!* he told himself. *God, I wish I could do something.* When he forced the dreamlike state to lift; the reality of what they faced settled over him like a heavy, dark cloud. He maybe could function, but it was a much harder place to be.

"What about my car?" Ben asked.

"Um . . . one of the other parents will drive it home, Ben," Nancy said. "Don't worry about the car now. I'll be up front if you need me, Boo."

The paramedics loaded Ben into the ambulance. As John and Nancy looked at each other, sadness and fear passed between them in a flash.

"Drive carefully, Honey," she said.

"What? Oh, yeah. Sure."

Nancy walked to the ambulance's front door as the back door closed. John pressed his hand against the glass in a gesture of hope, pain, and despair. He squeezed his lips together and looked at his son. Still motionless, Ben chatted with the attendant.

"I'll be right behind you, Ben!" he called through the door.

As the ambulance pulled away, Ben told the attendant about his golf game. "I enjoy hockey, but I really love golf." He called to his mother, "I used to have a beautiful golf swing, didn't I, Mom?"

"Yes, you did, Ben." Nancy immediately regretted her answer. It was in the past tense.

JOHN RAN TO HIS CAR, opened the door, got in, and sat motionless. *Now what? What'll happen if Ben can't walk or move? What's that called? Quadriplegic? Oh, God, no!*

He started the car, shifted gears, and drove out of the parking lot. He hated being alone, particularly at that moment. He wished someone, anyone, was with him. He lived his life surrounded by friends and family. Other people gave him strength. Suddenly, when he probably needed people most, he was totally alone. His only companion was the deep sense of foreboding.

His mind had only one focus: Ben. He raced to catch up with the ambulance. Without thinking, he sped through stop signs and red lights. *I have to stay close. I'm right here, Benny!* He drove like a man possessed. Afterward, he had no memory of the long drive to the hospital.

Instinctively, he reached for his cell phone, wondering who to call, but knowing he should let people know what had happened. His parents were in

Florida. He mentally went through a checklist of his friends. *I have to talk to someone,* he thought.

He spent the next twenty minutes speaking to friends as he drove to the hospital. As he described the accident, he allowed himself to be caught up in wondering about the future and reliving the past.

Guilt began to slip into his brain. He had been the one to get Ben interested in hockey. *Why did I introduce Ben to that damn game?* he wondered. *Why didn't I let him concentrate on golf? He loves golf, and he's a better golfer than a hockey player anyway. And hockey's so damn rough. He wasn't planning to play college hockey, anyway. I should've let him quit.* A realization chilled his mind. *He stuck it out for me. I know it. He wasn't big enough. No matter how hard he tried, the other kids were stronger. It's all my fault.*

John made a few more calls while berating himself for what had happened to his son. He called his good friend, Michael O'Rourke, and explained what had happened.

"How bad is it?" Michael asked.

"I don't know. He couldn't move, though."

"Maybe it's only temporary, like a severe shock that will subside." Michael's calm voice and clear logic broke through the dark cloud of fear and guilt enough to give John some alternate thoughts.

Of course, John told himself. *It's probably a temporary paralysis. Quit thinking about all the bad things that might happen. I don't know crap about his condition, and I'm already thinking the worst.*

"Thanks, Michael," he said to his friend. "I'll bet you're right. It's probably just temporary. Okay, I'm at the hospital now, so I'd better hang up. I'll call later with a progress report."

"We'll pray for him. Call me soon."

NANCY'S MIND WANDERED as she listened to her son chat almost nonstop with the ambulance attendant. She sensed it was a mistake to dwell on the negatives that hung over their heads, but, for the moment, she was helpless to control her own thoughts, and they dove deeply into fear.

Is this it? she wondered, looking at the immobile form of her seventeen-year-old son. *He looks so frail and helpless. I'm so afraid for him and John, not to mention Annie. How will I tell my parents? They'll be devastated. What about my faith? My beliefs? Are they strong enough to sustain me? I hope for the best, but God help me, I fear the worst. Is God with us now?*

"How are you doing, Boo?" she asked as calmly as she could manage, trying to hide her fears.

"I'm okay, Mom. You know when I was lying on the ice . . . I thought my arms and legs were above my head. Isn't that weird? Then, I thought I couldn't finish playing the game. I felt stupid lying there. I started thinking about the football player who was paralyzed last fall. He was hit harder than me, though. I don't think I was hit that hard. I'll bet they'll let me go home tonight. This is just shock or something. What do you think?"

14

Again Nancy lifted her voice above her own distress. "I don't know, Boo. Let's try not to worry about it until we talk to the doctors, okay?" She tried to sound hopeful, but she feared her voice gave her away even with effort.

Nancy remembered looking into Ben's eyes as he lay on the ice. They were so expressive and full of life. Whatever happened, Ben would remain himself. That thought gave Nancy her first comfort. Ben was bright, personable, had a great sense of humor. Somehow, no matter what, he'd make the best of things. He would be challenged, maybe, but he'd always have his mind.

It was a little early for the fears to give up. *Yes, but . . . What if . . . ? What if he's confined to a bed for the rest of his life? What if John and I have to care for him until . . . ? Stop it! Ben deserves more than that.*

"Mom, what about Annie? Does she know yet? Isn't she playing at Braemar this afternoon?"

Nancy swallowed and tried again to control her voice. "Casey drove her to the game. He'll bring her back to the house. Don't worry about it." Leave it to him to worry about his sister. Then she remembered. *Today is Annie's thirteenth anniversary! Thirteen years ago, I went to Bogota to pick her up from the orphanage.* In the heat of moment, she had entirely forgotten.

It seemed ironic.

The ambulance arrived at the emergency-room entrance and stopped. The rear doors opened as Nancy got out. She watched the paramedics unload Ben and wheel him through the doors. Looking

15

around, she saw John parking the car a short distance away, so she waved and followed Ben.

Once inside, the attendants wheeled him into a vacant room. Doctors and nurses converged on Ben from all directions. John joined his wife. They hugged and held hands, clinging to each other as they stood to the side. The smell of antiseptic permeated the small space, adding an exclamation point to the tension.

A nurse appraoched them. "Are you the parents?" she asked.

"Yes," John said, wrenching his attention from Ben, praying for good news.

"Why don't you stand over there for now?" She pointed to a corner of the room near the opening of the curtain.

John and Nancy moved to where she had showed them and watched the nurses remove Ben's skates, cut off his jersey, breezers, shoulder pads, elbow pads, socks, and shin pads.

When Nancy looked at Ben's expression, it was clear he was terrified. She felt her blood churning, coursing through her veins like steam in a high-pressure hose. Her ears rang. She wondered what was happening. So far no one was telling them anything; they had become bystanders in this hospital drama.

Those attending Ben moved him very carefully, going about their business with efficiency and grave concern. As if they shared only one expression in their work, all white-jacketed members of the staff looked grim.

John and Nancy overheard snatches of short, staccato phrases, all referring to spinal cord injury and trauma.

. The words had an electrifying effect on them, sounding worse even than their secret fears when spoken aloud. Then they heard the one word they most feared? Paralyzed. John gasped, and Nancy put her arm around him.

John felt as if he had turned to stone. Unlike his wife, blood didn't race through him. It drained from his face, and he felt totally lifeless.

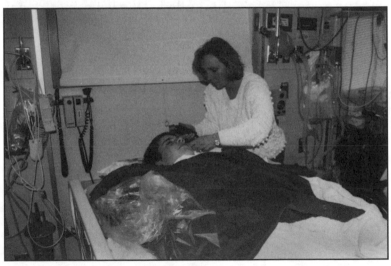

Methodist Hospital Emergency Room.

They were transfixed in their confined space. The doctors were very businesslike. Unlike previous trips to emergency rooms to repair cuts and broken bones, John and Nancy felt nervous tension as the

17

staff worked. They heard no idle conversation, no sharing of stories about someone's indiscretion or misadventure. The mood in the room remained completely businesslike and somber.

Nancy kept telling herself not to panic. *Wait and see*, she thought.

Another nurse approached them. "It would be best if you waited outside. There's a small waiting room just down the hall. Someone will be out to speak with you shortly." She returned to Ben's side.

John felt sick as he took his wife's hand and left the room. "Ben?" he called. "We'll be just down the hall, okay?"

Sedated, Ben was only half-conscious. "Uh . . . yeah, Dad. Okay." He stared at the bright lights over his head.

John and Nancy knew he wasn't okay. He hadn't suffered "a little shock" and wouldn't be leaving with them in a few hours to go home and sleep off the effects of the game's hard check. Walking out of that emergency cubicle, leaving Ben in the doctors' care, the Peytons walked away with the grim knowledge that they all faced a long road.

"BEN?" A DOCTOR ASKED. "Can you hear me?"

"Uh . . . yes . . ." the teen said.

"We have to attach a metal device to your head. I'll give you a series of injections in your scalp to numb the tissue. You should feel only a slight pinprick. Okay?"

"Sure. What's it look like?"

The doctor held it up, and Ben was surprised to see it had screws in it. That was his first hint of the seriousness of his injury, and he felt frightened. His mind began racing out of control.

I may never walk again, he thought. *No more golf, hunting, or anything. What about Dad? Will he want to spend time with me if I . . . if I'm in a wheelchair and can't move? How will he handle this? It'll be harder on him than on Mom.* Tired and scared he didn't know what to think.

"Where are my parents?" he asked with difficulty.

"They're just down the hall. They'll be in as soon as we're finished."

Chapter Two

Catastrophic Impairment

T HE TWO DISTRAUGHT PARENTS walked the short distance to the waiting room and huddled together. John, feeling nauseated by all that had happened, lowered his head between his knees.

"Are you all right, Honey?" Nancy asked.

He took a deep breath and looked up. "I . . . guess so." His voice shook. "Did I push him too hard, Nance?"

Nancy knew immediately what ran through her husband's mind. She had felt a long parade of doubt herself. "No! Ben would never have kept playing if he didn't want to. You know that."

"I shouldn't have cared about it so much, though. He wanted to quit last fall. He said he hated going into corners, that he was afraid of being run into the boards, getting hit hard and maybe becoming par . . ." He couldn't say the word. After a moment, he continued, "I knew a long time ago he'd never be more than an average hockey player. He wasn't big or strong enough, and he didn't care about the game that much. Golf was his first love. I should've left him alone."

"John, this isn't helping. You can't blame yourself for what happened. Or anyone else, either."

"I can't help it. I skated with Ben and his buddies. He disliked how rough the game's gotten almost as much as I did. You know as well as I do that if a kid doesn't make varsity by his junior year, he probably never will. Ben told me he wanted to keep playing because of his buddies. He loved the joking and camaraderie."

"Yes, and that was his choice. We have to stop this guilt and blame right now. Promise me no more. We can't think about the future or the past. We won't go there. Stay in the moment. I want to deal with what's in front of us right now, okay?"

John sighed. If he thought he was to blame, he didn't know what he'd do. "What if he never walks again, Nance? What if he's a quad . . ." He looked at her, tears streaming down his face. Then he reached for her.

Nancy put her arms around him, and together, they unburdened their hearts with quiet, private tears for a long time. Finally, they ran out. At least for the moment. A sense of gentle calm enveloped Nancy. She felt God with her.

She sat back, wiped her eyes, and asked, "Do the numbers one and thirty mean anything to you?"

John blinked. "No. Why?"

"I don't know. The clock on the scoreboard read one-thirty when Ben lay on the ice." She closed her eyes, trying to remember where she saw those numbers before.

She reached into her coat pocket and pulled out a folded piece of paper, opening it and staring at the words on the page without speaking. Finally, she said, "Oh, my God."

"What's the matter?"

"Do you remember the sermon this morning? It was the Angel's message." She looked at the crinkled paper.

John had trouble following her. "The sermon? Yes. There was something about not being afraid, or words to that effect." The service seemed such a long time ago.

"Yes. It was an Advent sermon. Look. It's here in the church bulletin. Wait." She picked up a Bible conveniently placed on the end table. "Listen to this. 'And the Angel said unto her, fear not Mary, for thou hast found favor with God.' That's it. It's Luke chapter one, verse thirty. One-thirty."

John stared at her in awe. Her memory was unbelievable, especially when it came to her spiritually. He wondered what the coincidence meant.

"I don't know what this means," she said slowly, "except that if we're going to get through this, we have to get past our fears about Ben. God's message is clear. Ben has God's grace, and we shouldn't be frightened. Even if he never moves again, we still have his essence, his spirit. Did you see his eyes when he was on the ice? That's our Ben. His life, energy, hopes, and dreams were in his eyes. Nothing can take that from him. God's telling us to have faith, that whatever happens, Ben will still be Ben."

John listened intently. He was a spiritual man, but he wasn't as vocal about his faith or as studied as his wife. Something in her words stirred a new awareness in him. More than anything, he needed something to ground him, to hang onto. After twenty-five years of marriage, Nancy still managed to amaze him. He looked at her and smiled.

She smiled back. "No matter what, Honey, we'll always have our son."

"Okay. Let's promise not to get too far ahead of ourselves. We'll deal with what we know. The future will take care of itself."

Nancy smiled her agreement.

"Mr. and Mrs. Peyton?"

John and Nancy's heads snapped up to see a man in the doorway of the waiting room.

"I'm Dr. Haines. I'm a pediatric neurosurgeon. I'd like to talk to you about your son." The man's words echoed in the small room as he approached and sat across from them.

"How is he?" John asked.

"Your son has suffered a very serious injury. His spinal cord is bruised. Certain vertebrae are dislocated. We're attempting to stabilize the spinal column with sandbags. Normally, we try to stretch the vertebrae back into place through traction.

"We won't know the real extent of his injuries until he has an MRI. He has no reflexive movement from the shoulders down. There's undoubtedly swelling around the spinal cord, and we're treating that with steroids. The damage seems confined to the third through sixth cervical vertebrae." He paused, pointing to a chart showing the spinal cord.

The doctor's initial report on Ben's condition was grim.

Nancy looked at John, who was pale again, and more tears showed in his eyes. She turned back to the doctor. "What else?"

"Unfortunately, our MRI equipment is down. We can't perform the tests here. I suggest we transfer him to University Hospital as soon as possible. I must tell you that the first thirty-six hours after an injury of this magnitude are the most critical. Generally, the outcome of his condition will make itself known during that time. It's important to move quickly on this. Ben has been stabilized and is without pain. Do you have any questions?"

John tried not to panic. It was happening too fast. The doctor's words stunned him. He had known Ben's injury was serious when it first happened, but he just wished the doctor had offered some words of reassurance or hope. It would have been wonderful if he had told them not to worry. He hadn't. "I'm sure we'll have more questions later, Doctor. Nance?"

Nancy, feeling strangely calm, unfolded her hands and stood. "No. Thank you, Doctor. We'd like to see our son now."

"Very well," Dr. Haines said, also standing. "I must warn you that we had to immobilize Ben's head. You'll see a metal halo with screws leading to his skull. We numbed the area. He's in no pain, but it might frighten you."

John knew Ben's ordeal was just beginning.

They walked into the room. Nancy was prepared for what she saw, but John wasn't. She smiled as she went to the gurney. "Hi, Sweetie. Looks like they've got you bound up and ready to go. How do you feel?"

John just stared with his hand over his mouth, then he turned away. It was too much. He couldn't take any more, but he couldn't let Ben see him like that, either.

As Ben and Nancy chatted, John steeled himself and walked back to the gurney. "Hi, Boo. How ya doin', Buddy?"

"Hi, Dad. Okay, I guess. I'm kinda groggy. What did the doctors say? Will I walk?" His voice was filled with fear.

"It's too soon to know, Boo," Nancy said with motherly assurance. "We need to get you to University Hospital for an MRI. Then we'll know more."

"Mom? I want to go home." Tears welled in Ben's eyes.

Nancy wanted nothing more than to take him home, wrap her arms around him, and tell him everything would be all right, but she couldn't. She looked deeply into Ben's eyes, willing him the strength he needed to conquer his fear.

"Okay, folks," a nurse said, "the ambulance is here. We're ready to go."

"Mom, are you coming with me?" Ben asked.

Nancy looked at John. "They said there won't be room this time, Boo. Your dad and I will be right behind you, though. We'll be there." Her cheeks flushed. Blood surged through her veins, reoxygenated and energized from her lungs. The empathy she felt for her stricken son was unrelenting. Every vessel in her body hummed with energy and vigor for him. She wished she could give him something other than her love to make him better.

"We'll be right with you, Honey," she said.

The attendants came in and wheeled Ben down the hall to the ambulance. John and Nancy walked with him, each with one hand on his chest. They stood side by side as he was loaded into the vehicle. Ben's eyes were closed.

Both parents said good-bye and walked to John's car. It was snowing, and six inches of fluffy, heavy snow accumulated on top of the three feet they already had that winter. At twenty degrees, it was a typical December day in Minnesota.

Neither spoke for the first five minutes. Finally, John asked, "Do you think Annie's home by now?"

Nancy glanced at her watch. "It's three forty-five. Her game ended at three. She should be at the Hankinsons."

"When will we tell her?"

"Let's wait until we know more."

"I guess." John's mind was wandering. He was letting himself get too far ahead, and didn't want that.

"What are you thinking about?"

"I don't know. I'm trying not to think ahead, but I can't seem to stop. The sight of that metal thing attached to his head freaked me out. I don't know. This is all too hard . . ." He began crying quietly.

"Pull over, Honey."

John pulled onto a side street in south Minneapolis and stopped. Snow fell more heavily than before. Nancy slid over and put her arms around him, letting him cry awhile. He sobbed, feeling anguished when faced with the grim reality that his son might never walk again or even be able to feed himself.

Nancy cried, too. In the privacy of their car, they allowed themselves a brief interlude to express the pain that had been building all afternoon. Out of sight of their injured son, they gave in to their sorrow. Other low points would come. Both knew that the moment in the car wasn't their last.

Then it was over. They straightened up, wiped away their tears and mentally prepared for the long, agonizing, fearful days to come.

"If we give in to our fears, we won't be there for Ben," Nancy said. "Somehow, we'll find peace and serenity if we stay in the moment. Remember, Ben will always be Ben."

John nodded and took a deep breath. "Yes, he will. Now I know how other parents feel who've had a tragedy with a child. I never experienced anything like this before. Nothing so close. Mom and Dad are still with us. I've been lucky."

"That reminds me. We have to call our parents. They'll be devastated by this. Ben's close to all four of them. Should we call now or later?"

"I want to wait to call Mom and Dad."

"I need to get it over with. I don't want to make this call, but I have to." Picking up the cell phone, she dialed her parents' number. Her mother answered after a few rings.

They exchanged pleasantries, then Nancy said, "Mom, I have bad news."

John drove as Nancy broke the news to her parents. He'd never felt so depressed or heartsick in his life and wondered how much worse it could get.

"We're at the hospital now, Mom," Nancy said. "I have to go. I'll call later. Yes, I will. We love you, too. Bye." She hung up and stared out the window.

John cast her a concerned glance. "Nance? Are you all right?"

Nancy sighed. "Oh, John, that was so hard. I don't think she took it very well, either." Nancy knew she had to stay strong and focused in the moment, but it was so difficult. She said, "No one could possibly prepare for this."

"I can't imagine how," John said quietly.

They arrived at the University of Minnesota Hospital, one of the best critical-care facilities in the state, especially for patients with spinal cord injuries. They parked and entered the emergency room.

As they walked in, a nurse asked, "Mr. and Mrs. Peyton? Ben's already undergoing the MRI. Dr. Haines would like to speak with you as soon as he's read the results. If you'd like, there's a waiting room over there." She pointed.

Another waiting room, John thought morosely, walking to the phone to call his friend, Dr. Roby Thompson. He needed confirmation that Dr. Haines was the best available physician for Ben.

John returned a few minutes later. "Roby said Ben's in good hands. Dr. Haines is the preeminent surgeon in his field. We're fortunate to have him on Ben's case."

"Good. That's one less thing to worry about."

They sat. They still hadn't heard a precise description of Ben's injury, only speculation. They needed solid, concrete answers. They didn't wait long.

Dr. Steven Haines knocked on the door, then entered. All three huddled together as the doctor pulled out a chart for reference.

Nancy searched the doctor's eyes for a glimmer of hope, but all she saw was that same serious, concerned frown that had marked everyone's expression.

"I'll try to go slowly," Dr. Haines said, "but I must tell you that we need to get Ben into surgery as quickly as possible." He pointed to a picture of the spinal cord. "Ben suffered a very serious trauma to the vertebral column, also known as the spine. Specifically, the damage is confined to the C3 through C6 cervical vertebrae, shown here." He pointed to the vertebrae in question. "The MRI shows swelling and bone fragments that have to be removed. I'm fairly certain that the fifth vertebrae has impended into and over the fourth. Normally, we'd wait for the swelling to recede, but, in your son's case, we must operate immediately.

He changed the angle of the chart. "We'll enter from the back, or posterior. We'll remove the bone chips, surgically relocate the fourth and fifth vertebrae, and fuse three through six with donor bone. I must tell you this is a very delicate operation, and there is a great deal of risk."

He paused to let his words sink in.

The tension in the room hummed.

"What . . . what kind of risk?" John asked, fearing the answer.

"The spinal cord carries thirty-one pairs of nerves that branch out to all parts of the body. It's important that you understand that if the pathway on any of those nerves is interrupted, that part of the body doesn't receive the designated signals from the brain, and it ceases to function. All the nerves below the injury no longer carry impulses to their respective body parts."

He paused again before continuing. "When that happens, neural conduction ceases. In Ben's case, damage to the fourth and fifth vertebrae and respective nerve endings could cause partial or total cessation of all movement below his shoulders. Partial recovery is possible but not likely. We won't know the extent of the injury until we get in and look, but I want to prepare you for the ultimate outcome."

He glanced at his watch. John and Nancy had trouble comprehending all he had said, but the implications sounded grave. The impact of his words rang in their ears. For a moment, neither had the courage to ask the one question they most wanted answered.

As if reading their minds, Dr. Haines said, "A spinal-cord injury is a catastrophic impairment and is always accompanied by some sort of paralysis, disability, and handicap. I know those are frightening and terrifying words to hear, but I would be remiss if I didn't spell it out for you. Having said all that, I am hopeful we can retard some of the damage by stabilizing the spine and the bruised cord."

"Could it be that only one or two vertebrae are damaged, not all four?" John asked.

"That's entirely possible," said Dr. Haines. "I can only tell you what the worst case might be at this point. Anything less than that will be a plus. I must confess that I'm surprised at the severity of the injury. We don't see many hockey injuries like this unless the player went into the boards head first. Are you certain Ben wasn't hit earlier?"

"He complained yesterday about being hit with a high stick around the neck," John said. "He said his neck was stiff and sore last night, but I didn't pay much attention. He considered not playing this morning, but, after a hot shower, he said he felt better. Do you think that was a contributing factor?"

The doctor considered. "It's possible. Yesterday's injury could have weakened the tissue to the extent that, when he was hit again today, the muscles couldn't stave off the blow." He looked at his watch. "It's five-thirty. You should prepare for a long evening. I expect the operation will take five to six hours. I know I've thrown a lot at you, and I apologize for that.Do you have any questions?"

John and Nancy looked at each other. The doctor's words had struck hard. They felt as if a large piece of plaster had fallen from the ceiling onto their heads. Both were staggered, not knowing what to say.

"Okay, then," Dr. Haines said. "I'll leave this brochure with you. It should answer some questions.

One of the nurses will come out occasionally to give you progress reports."

Nancy accepted the pamphlet from the doctor, though neither parent had the courage to read its graphic, too-descriptive contents. "Can we see Ben now?"

"Certainly. He's groggy, but I'll take you to him."

When they entered the room, they were stunned. Ben was attached to a variety of monitors, and IV tubes ran to both wrists. A single stark, white sheet covered his damaged body. The room was filled with nurses, prepping him for surgery.

Nancy sighed and walked closer. "Ben? Can you hear me?"

Ben slowly opened his eyes and tried to focus. He heard her, but he had trouble seeing her. "Mom? What's going to happen? The docs didn't say much. If they did, I don't remember."

"Dr. Haines is going to operate on you, Boo. He needs to relieve the swelling along your spine and make sure everything is stable." She didn't want to say more.

"How long will it take?"

"Oh, a few hours, I guess." She nodded to John, wishing him closer.

"Ben?" John asked. "Can you hear me, Buddy?"

"Huh? Oh, hi, Dad."

The anesthetist looked up. "We need to take him now, folks. You can walk with him partway if you like."

The attendants wheeled Ben from the room and down the long hall. John walked beside him in a daze. The nightmare of the long day continued.

Nancy watched her son's face as she walked, tears forming in her eyes and slipping gently down each red cheek. As they reached the door to surgery, she leaned over to kiss his forehead. "I love you, Ben. See you soon." She reached down to wipe her tears from his face.

John stepped forward and kissed Ben, too. "We'll be right outside, Boo. I love you, son."

They watched the gurney pass through the doors. Then Ben was gone. Nancy felt as if nothing in the world could make her feel better. She couldn't comfort her son or be with him. All she could do was pray.

They turned and walked hand in hand toward the surgical waiting room to begin their long vigil.

SOMETIME LATER, AFTER JOHN and Nancy couldn't endure being alone any longer, she called John's parents.

"I know," she said. "Yes. We will. What? No. That's okay. Go ahead and tell me." She listened intently. "Oh, Betty. I don't know what to say. No, that's perfectly all right. We'll keep this to ourselves for now. Give Morrow a hug. Bye." She hung up and turned to John. "You'll never guess what happened."

"What?"

"You remember how your mother keeps a special ornament for each child and grandchild on their Christmas tree?"

John's face tightened. Hesitantly, he said, "Yes. Do I want to hear this?"

"I think you do. This morning, as she walked by the tree, she heard a noise. The ornament that was Ben's, a little hockey player, fell off and landed on the floor."

John looked at her, wondering what to say. "That sounds, well, ominous, doesn't it?"

"Yes. I wish she hadn't told me. I need to talk to Annie. I won't frighten her any more than necessary."

"Good idea."

Annie Peyton.

Shortly after talking with her mom, Annie walked the short distance from the Hankinsons' house to her own home. Her friend JJ and his parents would pick her up soon, but she had to pack a small bag and feed the pets first. The two golden retrievers, Winnie, age twelve, and Phoebe, age one, greeted her at the door.

Oliver, Annie's little fluffy white dog, no bigger than a baseball glove, jumped up and down in excitement as Annie walked into the house. The two cats, Herbie and Ralph, sauntered by with hardly a glance in her direction.

"Hi, guys. I'll bet you're all hungry." She played with the dogs, took them out for a short walk, and returned to the house to feed them.

Just as she finished, a horn honked outside.

"Oops! That'll be the Kortans. I gotta go. Gimme a kiss, you guys." Leaning down, she hugged the two larger dogs, then picked up Oliver and kissed his muzzle before setting him down. After locking the door behind her, she ran to the car.

Annie and the Kortans were having dinner at a local restaurant. Annie still didn't know how serious Ben's injury was, only that he had been hurt and taken to the hospital. The idea of a broken leg still in her head, she hadn't gotten very upset as yet. Halfway through their meal, however, an acquaintance approached the table and stood behind Annie.

"Did you hear about Ben?" he asked. "He broke his neck playing hockey today."

Annie set down her fork, looked at her friend, JJ, and burst into tears. Her world shattered. She had thought Ben would be home the following day.

The Kortans tried to console her, but the damage had been done. Annie and her brother were like any two siblings four years apart in age. They fought and got in each other's way, but they also loved each other.

Annie looked up and said quietly, "I want to go home now."

"Of course, Annie," Mrs. Kortan said. "Your mother wants you to spend the night with us tonight. I'll take you to the hospital in the morning, okay?"

Annie stood, left the table, and walked out of the restaurant.

AS EVENING BECAME NIGHT, the waiting room for non-family members slowly began filling. John and Nancy wouldn't learn until much later that many good friends came early that evening to wait, hope, and pray.

The people who gathered shared what they knew of Ben's condition. They passed the time discussing John and Nancy and their injured son. By nine o'clock, word reached the Peytons that the room upstairs was filled with concerned friends waiting for word about Ben.

They were shocked and surprised. Neither one had considered the possibility that many of their friends knew about the injury or that they would come to the hospital on a Sunday night two days before Christmas. The stressed couple decided they'd been alone with their fears long enough and told the nurse they were moving to the other, larger room. They went upstairs to wait with their caring, concerned friends.

Friends and relatives join the Peytons for the long wait.

When they joined their friends, their circle of support formed. Like a pebble tossed casually into still water, ripples moved out, broadening the circle.

As they entered the room, they greeted each in turn with hugs of affection. John told them what they knew of Ben's condition.

Nancy looked around the large, open room, filled with an assortment of comfortable chairs and sofas. There were plenty of refreshments, too. Still, the room was poorly lit and cold. The only warmth came from their friends, not the heating system.

They sat in small groups or paced as they waited for further word about Ben.

A nurse, who came in at ten o'clock, spoke with John and Nancy. "They found more swelling and bone chips than anticipated, but the surgery is going well."

"How much longer?" Nancy asked.

"Another few hours, I'd say," the nurse told them. "Any other questions?"

"How's he doing?" John asked.

"He's a strong boy. He's got youth on his side, and he's in great condition. He's doing well. We'll keep you apprised of any changes. I'd better get back now."

"Thank you," John and Nancy said in unison.

They returned to the waiting room to relay the news to their friends. After that, everyone settled down to wait.

"What are you thinking, Morrie?" Michael asked John.

"Huh? Oh. Sorry. I was thinking about how much Ben loved golf. I don't know. Do you remember that quote about playing the ball where it lies? It seems appropriate right now."

"Have you guys ever seen Ben swing a golf club?" Peter, another friend, asked, hoping to lighten the tone ·of the conversation.

"Smoothest swing I ever saw," Hank said. "He spends all his free time playing golf. He'll play with anyone, anytime."

"That's true," John said to the men. "The old guys love playing with him. He chats 'em up and tells jokes they haven't heard before. They argue about who gets to play with him, because they know it's money in their pockets."

1995. Father and son together, playing the game both loved.

The others laughed at the image of young Ben spending his summer weekends playing with the white-haired, retired set.

There were additional attempts to lighten the mood. For the most part, though, the seriousness of Ben's situation constantly intruded, bringing such topics to silence. After a while, though, the conversation turned to the accident.

"How do you feel about the kid who hit him?" Hank asked.

"I haven't even thought about him," John said immediately. "It seems like a waste of energy to spend much time blaming him or anyone else. You all know how rough the game has gotten. Yes, it was an illegal check, but I've seen Ben get hit harder. I can't blame the other kid. If you asked Ben, he'd say the same thing. Hank, you've had three sons play hockey, first in high school, then at the U. What do you think?"

"The game's a lot different now from when you and Peter played. I wish it wasn't because something's been lost. Maybe it's the beauty and flow of the game. It used to be that stick handling, passing, and skating were a larger part of the game. Now, those skills are rare. What you see now is a lot of clutching, grabbing, stick work on the body, and too much hitting. According to Morrie, Ben was hit the night before. That may've had something to do with this."

"What do you mean?" Peter asked.

"Ben was in a game on Saturday night," John replied, "and some kid slashed him pretty hard high on the left side of the neck. Nancy and I were at a Christmas party and didn't see the game. When we got home, Annie told us some parents called to ask about Ben. They were worried. He went down like he'd been pole-axed."

"What did Ben say?" Michael asked.

"Oh, you know Ben. He dismissed it, said only that his neck was sore. He admitted he had trouble sleeping, but he wanted to play on Sunday because it was the championship game."

"Did you tell the doctor?" Hank asked.

"Yeah, I did. It might have only been speculation on his part, but he thought it might've weakened the muscles. When Ben was hit today, he couldn't protect himself. I don't know. Maybe it doesn't make any difference. He's been hit a lot in the past. Saturday's thing just seemed like another minor bruise." John forced himself not to pursue the subject.

"Have you and Nancy had anything to eat?" Bill asked, hoping to change the subject.

"I haven't even thought about food," John said, looking toward his wife, who sat with her friends. "Nance? Are you hungry?"

She turned. "No. Not really. Maybe I'll get a sandwich in a little while. I'm okay right now."

ANOTHER CLOSE FRIEND who was also a minister, Karla McGraw, arrived at eleven o'clock. She took one look around the room, and said to Nancy, "Behold the faces of God."

Nancy was moved to tears by her friend's statement. "Thank you, Karla." Nancy dried her eyes and hugged her friend tightly.

"You're going to see many more of your friends and neighbors over the next few days. They'll all want to share your pain and comfort you. Interestingly, they'll leave feeling comforted."

God is love, Nancy thought. *He's here right now, in this cold, poorly lit room.*

The multiple conversations ended, and the others focused on the gentle woman standing with Nancy.

"Know what?" Nancy asked her friend. "I'd like to pray. Karla, would you mind?"

"Not at all. Why don't we all stand together?"

They stood and gathered around Karla, Nancy, and John, holding hands and bowing their heads. Karla opened with the Lord's Prayer and finished with a blessing for the attending doctors and an appeal for Ben's health and safety.

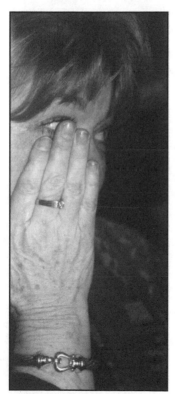

Tears of gratitude.

"Amen," everyone said.

"Thank you all for being here," Nancy said. "You'll never know how much this means to John and me."

"Yes," John said with feeling. "You're all good friends. I didn't want to bother any of you, with it being Christmas and all, but I have to admit I'm glad . . . I . . . did . . ." He couldn't finish. After a moment, he looked around and said, "Thank you."

At eleven-thirty, one of their pastors called. Nancy spoke with him for a long time. When she returned to the waiting room, tears ran down her cheeks.

43

"Nance? What's wrong?" John asked.

"I'm sorry. These are tears of gratitude." She wiped her eyes. "That was Pastor Stark. Someone apparently initiated a telephone tree tonight to announce an impromptu prayer vigil for Ben at Christ Presbyterian Church. Reverend Stark said that normally, he opens the chapel for twenty or thirty people. Tonight, he had over six hundred! There were friends, neighbors, classmates, business associates, and Ben's teammates. Can you imagine?"

John stared. "I can't believe it."

Nancy looked around the room. *We aren't alone with our sorrow. Thank You, God.*

Chapter Three

In the Moment

Decemeber 22, the winter solstice, the shortest day of
the year, yet one that seemed interminable, finally
ended as the clock's hands inched past midnight.
For the Peytons, another long day began.

John and Nancy waited patiently and hopefully with
their friends for word of their son. Surgery was still in
progress at one o'clock. Although outwardly calm, the
Peytons' concern and worry grew with each passing minute.

Is this it? Nancy wondered. *Is this our ultimate test as
parents? If so, what'll sustain us? Will our beliefs see us
through?*

Then, as she looked at everyone else in the room dozing or quietly chatting, she reminded herself, *Don't look too far ahead. Stay in the moment.*

That simple thought felt good.

Dr. Haines walked into the waiting room at 2:15. He took John and Nancy aside to give them the news.

"The surgery went well," he said. "I did a good job. The next twelve hours will indicate if we were as successful as I hope. We need to ascertain that the vertebral column is stable, and the swelling diminishes rapidly. Once we were in, we realized that most of the damage was to the fourth and fifth vertebrae. We separated them, removed the bone fragments, and fused the third, fourth, fifth and sixth vertebrae."

"What's next?" John asked.

"We watch, wait, hope, and pray. It's too early to determine the level of permanent damage, but it doesn't look good. As I said earlier, this type of trauma almost always brings loss of feelings in the legs and perhaps the arms. If Ben's going to move anything below his shoulders, it'll happen some time in the next thirty-six hours. It would be wise to prepare yourselves, and Ben when the time is right, for what he can expect. His final disability level will likely be fairly extensive."

"Will he ever walk again?" John blurted.

"Not unless . . ." Dr. Haines pointed toward the ceiling.

John felt like he'd been kicked in the stomach by a mule. He had hoped not to hear words like "disability" or "paralysis" but now "permanent?" The reality of it was staggering. He walked slowly toward the other side of the hall.

"I'm sorry, Mr. Peyton. Remember that Ben is strong, athletically fit, and, if his spirit is as strong as his body, well, miracles do happen."

"Thank you, Doctor," Nancy said. "Will we see you later?"

"Me? No. I'm going home. I need to get some sleep. They'll be checking Ben every hour, though." He turned to leave.

"One more thing . . ." Hesitation filled Nancy's voice. "I . . . don't know . . ." She shook her head. "Never mind."

Dr. Haines returned to her side and put his arm around her shoulders. "Are you sure? You can ask anything you want."

"No. Thank you." *Could he . . . die?* When she mentally formed the words, she blanched, and her lower lip quivered.

"Nance?" John asked. "Honey? What's wrong?"

She took a deep breath. "I'm okay. Really." Her voice shook with the words.

As if reading her mind, Dr. Haines said gently, "Let's deal with one thing at a time. You both have had a long, tortuous day. You need to go home and rest. It's important for you to keep up your strength, too. You'll need it." He squeezed Nancy's shoulder and left.

John, watching him walk away, remembered the fear in Nancy's voice. "Oh, God. Nance?" He looked at her in horror.

"No," she said adamantly. "We promised ourselves not to get too far ahead. We know all there is to know, and we've heard the risks. Ben is still in danger, but all we can do is deal with right now."

"I guess."

They walked back to the waiting room to tell their anxious friends most of what Dr. Haines said.

Encouraged by the report, their friends said good-bye and left. John and Nancy went to ICU to look at Ben. He was intubated, with a breathing tube running from his lungs to a ventilator. He would be unconscious for some time.

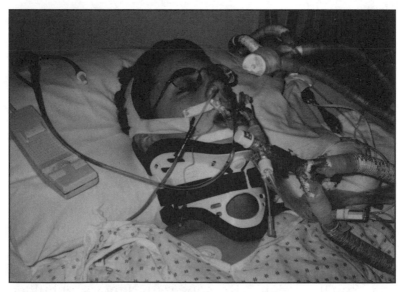

After the first surgery - intubated.

Each parent sat alone in the dark, lost in thoughts and fears. When it was time to go home, they kissed Ben and left for the long drive.

Both were too exhausted to speak once they were in the car. There was little or no traffic. Snow fell, but John made good time. Nancy laid back her head and closed her eyes. The only sound was the slapping of the wipers fighting the heavy, wet snow.

As they pulled into their garage, they saw Ben's car parked out front. Like a gray, silent, sentinel of sorrow, the snow-covered vehicle reminded them of one thing: Ben would never drive it again.

John stopped the car, turned off the ignition, and groaned as he opened the door. As they walked inside, they greeted the dogs and stood at the bottom of the stairs without moving.

Nancy looked up the stairs. As with Ben's car, those stairs only served to remind her of what would never be again. Ben would never again be able to walk to his room.

In the privacy of their own home, Nancy finally opened her soul and lamented all that appeared lost. Moaning, she held her stomach as she cried. Her wail of misery came from a heart that was as broken as her child's neck.

John hugged her, cried with her, and felt helpless to mouth any words to ease her pain or his own. Slowly, they climbed the stairs, passed Ben's empty room and went to bed.

John slept, but Nancy couldn't. She dozed, woke, cried, and finally, at dawn, gave up and got dressed. After putting on her coat and boots, she took the dogs for a long, cold walk in the fresh snow.

MONDAY, DECEMBER 23, the snow stopped. The plows were out, moving tons of snow from the streets. The banks along each boulevard had already been high with that winter's accumulation of snow, and parking places were hard to find. The Peytons returned to the hospital early.

Ben was conscious periodically, but he kept sliding back into a foggy, dreamlike state. The surgery had been very exhausting, and he was weak. John and Nancy watched him carefully. From the continuous reports of doctors and nurses, they knew Ben was struggling.

They spoke to Annie by phone; she would join them at the hospital later. Hundreds of friends and relatives called the hospital and the Peytons' home for updates on Ben's condition, though they received little information.

Whitney, John's brother, arrived and established a hotline to provide regular updates on Ben's condition. Calls to the Peyton home as well as John's office were forwarded to a special service he set up.

John and Nancy left Ben's side briefly at ten-thirty to get something to eat. When they returned thirty minutes later, they found the waiting room full of well-wishers. They were stunned.

They walked around the room, thanking all those who came. Many of their friends from the previous night had returned, and they remained for a long time. Some of Ben's close friends came, too. They would soon become regular fixtures around the ICU unit, along with other teens close to Ben.

As the Peytons chatted with the throng, a nurse came in and brought them to Ben's room. As they entered the room, they felt the increased charge of nervous energy. Doctors and nurses moved rapidly around their son's bed. When they saw Dr. Haines, they knew something was wrong. He walked over to them.

"What's wrong?" Nancy asked, glancing anxiously at Ben.

"The swelling hasn't gone down, and there's some bleeding. I'm afraid we'll have to operate again. Let's step outside. I'll explain."

Their steps were heavy as they reluctantly followed the doctor into a small room across the hall. Dr. Haines stood near a blackboard and found a piece of chalk. "We're going for anterior entry this time, from the front, to insert two titanium rods alongside the damaged vertebrae. Simultaneously, we'll complete the fusion begun last night. We hoped we wouldn't have to go in again, but I'm afraid we must. It's critical that the swelling go down. I'm sorry. We have no choice."

"How long will this take?" John asked quietly.

"Another five or six hours maybe. Once we're done, that'll be the extent of what we can do for him surgically. After that, the following thirty-six hours will determine everything."

The doctor tried to offer some support. "I know this is tough on both of you, but you have to remain positive and strong. It's important that you get rest and keep up your strength. Remember, Ben's a fighter. He's strong, an athlete, and has youth on his side. You need to be as strong for him as he is for you. If you have no more questions, I need to get prepped. I'll be out later."

As the doctor left, John and Nancy looked at each other in shock. "Good Lord," John said. "Am I dreaming this? We've been through this once already. Now again?"

"I know, but it's out of our control. We have to trust the doctors." *Is this God's will?* Nancy wondered. *I refuse to accept that. These things just happen. God is with us in good times and bad.*

Once again, in the privacy of that small room, they allowed tears to flow, but not for long. They couldn't afford to dwell on the gloom that dogged them. Ben depended on them. They dried their eyes, smiled briefly, and returned to Ben's room.

Ben was wheeled into surgery at noon. For the second time in less than a day, John, Nancy, Annie, and other caring people settled back to wait.

Their vigil was reinforced by a steady stream of friends. Some stayed the entire afternoon, while others came and went. New people helped pass the time, and Nancy noted the changes in their visitors from the moment they arrived until they left. As Karla McGraw had said, without exception, she saw that they left feeling better for coming.

"John?" she asked quietly.

"What is it?"

"Have you noticed how genuinely heartbroken most of these people are? I've never seen so many grown men cry."

John nodded. "I know. It's almost hitting them harder than the women."

John, unable to sit still, wandered in and out of the waiting room. He walked the halls, called his office, and tried to keep moving. Even though he and Nancy should've been exhausted, they kept going.

One doctor suggested to Nancy that she and John visit the hospital chaplain.

"How would I find him?" she asked a nurse.

The nurse smiled. "It's a she. Her name is Mary Chapin." The nurse gave directions.

They walked down a maze of corridors and doorways. "Why do you think the doctor told us to see this person?" Nancy asked.

"I don't know. Did the suggestion come out of the blue?"

"Yes. It was very strange, as if he thought we had to see her for some reason."

Before long, they were lost.

"Maybe we should forget it and return," John said.

"Maybe, but something tells me . . ." Nancy saw a woman approaching. "Excuse me, can you tell us how to find Mary Chapin?"

The woman smiled. "Yes. You've just found her. I'm Mary Chapin. How can I help you?"

Nancy explained their mission, and Mary said, "I'm glad you found me. I was just on my way out of the building to begin my vacation. Let's go into this room and talk about Ben, shall we?"

They spent thirty minutes with the soft-spoken, kind woman. She asked them about Ben and Annie and suggested they pray together. When they finished, Mary opened her Bible and said, "Let me read you something from Luke. This is chapter twelve, verse four. 'And I say unto you my friends, be not afraid of them that kill the body, and after that have no more that they can do.' Does that sound familiar?"

"Yes. We heard a similar message," Nancy said. "What day is this? Oh. It was yesterday. Luke chapter one, verse thirty. The Advent message to Mary also speaks of fearing not. I believe someone is trying to tell us something, Chaplain."

Mary laughed. "I believe you both understand the message. Fear in itself is paralyzing. It gets in the way of healing. Let God give you the peace and serenity you deserve. God bless you and your children."

After they left the office of the small, white-haired woman, John said, "Something just occurred to me. How'd she know Ben's name?"

Nancy met his eyes. "I don't know. She didn't know we were coming. Otherwise, she would've waited for us. She was almost . . . angelic . . . wasn't she?"

They returned to the waiting room, feeling better for visiting the gentle lady.

Chapter Four

In His Eyes

A fternoon stretched into evening, and by seven o'clock, the operation was over. Ben was taken to the recovery room, and Dr. Haines spoke with John and Nancy.

"The next thirty-six hours will tell the tale," he said. "We'll monitor him closely and watch for any sign of movement. Frankly, as I said last night, I don't expect anything except predictable spasticity, which is involuntary. Ben's on a ventilator again to help him breathe. That increases the volume of inspired air and decreases the work required for breathing. Hopefully, he can breathe on his own tomorrow."

"What can we expect, Doctor?" Nancy asked.

"Our first concern is for his immediate health. Respiratory problems can occur. Pneumonia is the biggest danger. You'll meet Dr. Marshall Hertz shortly. He's a pulmonary specialist. All we can do now is wait and pray."

"Thanks, Doctor," John said.

Dr. Haines left them alone. For a moment, they were too drained to do anything but collapse into two chairs and begin the long, difficult process of watching and praying for anything positive.

After a while, they went to be with Ben, and Annie joined them. She moved close to the bed, looking directly into his pale face. Ben opened his eyes briefly, looked at his sister, and smiled around the tube in his mouth.

"Mom! He looked at me and smiled!" she said.

John and Nancy stood beside her, but Ben's eyes had closed in deep sleep again.

"It was in his eyes," Annie said. "He'll be all right. I know it."

John and Nancy looked at each other, neither willing to quell their daughter's enthusiasm.

"I hope you're right, Sweetheart," Nancy said. *Our little, dark-haired angel,* she thought.

"Mom, you and Dad should've been at that prayer vigil last night," Annie said.

"I didn't know you were there," Nancy said.

"Yeah. The Kortans took me. I had to stand in back alone. It was kinda sad, though. Casey got up after a while and spoke."

"What did he say?" John asked.

"You know Casey. Everybody knows him, 'cause he plays hockey for the U. He's a neat guy, always happy-go-lucky. He said something like, 'I just want to remind everyone that Ben isn't dead. This isn't a wake.'"

"Did he really?" Nancy asked.

"Yeah. He changed the sad feeling in the church all by himself. Then he said, 'Let's also remember Annie.' I felt so embarrassed."

Carey Hankinson, Ben and Annie's role model and friend.

Casey is one of a kind, John thought. Ben and Annie idolized him.

He saw Nancy's eyes glistening, then she cleared her throat. "Why don't you and Annie go home, shower, and get something to eat? You can return later."

John realized what she was asking. "Yeah. That's probably a good idea. We'll take turns staying with Ben. I hate to leave, though."

"He'll be unconscious for quite a while, but I'd like to stay," Nancy said.

"Okay. I'll be back in a few hours." John put on his coat, and he and Annie left for home.

Nancy spent the following hours moving between Ben's room and the waiting room, where a constantly changing group of people came and went. She tried not to think about Dr. Haines' cautious words. It was important not to become lost in worrying about things that might not happen.

Ben was her son, however, and his condition was perilous.

BEN FINALLY WOKE LATER that night. His memory of the past few hours was hazy. He wore a brace on his neck that tipped his head back in an awkward position. Because he was intubated, he couldn't speak, drink, or eat and required constant supervision. Mucus had to be suctioned from deep in his throat. He was thirsty, tired, and confused. No part of his body moved.

He cast his eyes back and forth, trying to understand where he was and what had happened. *Some sort of operation,* he thought. *Spinal cord . . . Methodist? No, somewhere else. Mom?*

"Mmmm?" he mumbled.

Nancy looked up. For the first time since before the initial operation, she saw her son looking at her with eyes full of questions and fear. "Boo?" she said. "Hi, Sweetheart. Can you hear me?"

He blinked to show he understood.

"You're at University Hospital. They operated on your neck and spine, but now it's over. The nurse said all you can have is ice chips. Do you want some?"

He blinked again.

"I'll get the nurse. Be right back, Honey."

She returned quickly with a critical-care nurse.

"Ben?" the nurse asked. "I can't give you anything but ice chips for a while. Let's see if these help." She slipped small pieces of ice between his parched lips. "How's that? Your mom can give you more anytime you want, okay?"

Ben blinked at her.

With each passing minute of renewed lucidity, Ben's mind raced to catch up. For the most part, there was a huge void. He couldn't remember much of what happened.

For the next hour, Nancy patiently explained what happened. She knew he must have questions about his condition, including his ability to move or walk, but she avoided talking about that directly. She'd explain it in due time, but not right away.

She did her best to take his mind off everything, chatting about the friends who'd come to see him at the hospital. When she told him about the candlelight vigil with 600 people, he was deeply moved and blinked back a flood of tears.

Nancy wiped his eyes. "You didn't know you had that many friends, did you?"

Ben looked away. Although tired and worried, he wondered what she wasn't telling him. He knew he was having trouble breathing. If he were paralyzed like Christopher Reeve, would he ever breathe unassisted? Could he die?

No, he thought. *I can breathe . . . I think . . .*

"Mmmm?" Being unable to speak disturbed him. Being unable to ask any specific question bothered him more.

Nancy, alarmed by his tone, asked God for strength. "What is it, Sweetheart? I know you're frustrated. We have to figure out a way to communicate with you. Maybe the nurse has something we can use."

She looked directly into her son's frightened blue eyes. It was clear Ben was scared, and so was she. She told herself to remember the words, "Fear not."

Ben was tired and accepted the idea that they'd have to figure out some way to communicate. Maybe later. He closed his eyes and drifted into an exhausted sleep, a blessed reprieve.

JOHN AND ANNIE RETURNED to the hospital at nine-thir-
ty. Ben woke long enough to acknowledge their presence, then promptly fell asleep again. His parents
decided John should return home with Annie. Nancy
would stay in Ben's room for the remainder of the
night.

Alone with her son and her thoughts, Nancy
felt strangely calm and relaxed. Mary Chapin's
words returned to her as she slowly fell asleep, "Be
not afraid . . ."

THE FOLLOWING DAY WAS Christmas Eve. Ben was taken
off the ventilator and felt alert and excited at being
conscious and able to speak again. For the first time
in two days, he was aware of what happened around
him and was happy to receive visitors.

"Jell-O?" he asked. "I can eat Jell-O? Who'll
feed me? Annie?"

"Sure," she said. "I'll do it." She picked up the
bowl and slowly spooned green dessert into her
brother's mouth. Between spoonfuls, Annie recount-
ed all the friends who had come by.

The room filled with visitors, and Ben chatted
with everyone, eager to joke with his friends. *It was
neat they came to see me.* He was quickly learning the
meaning of gratitude.

It didn't take long for the small room to over-
flow with cards, flowers, and balloons, as well as
stuffed animals of every size and description. The
acute-care staff attended to his needs and patiently

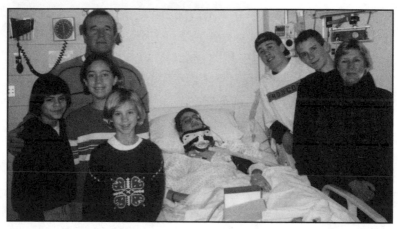

Uncle Jay and family visit from Colorado.

answered his questions. They explained the function
of the catheter, IVs, and EKG machines. They showed
him how they monitored his bodily functions and told
him someone was always watching over him.

On Christmas Eve, John and Nancy decided
that Annie needed to have a semblance of Christmas.
She and her father would leave and spend the evening
with the Hankinson family. Nancy would stay with Ben.
When he slept, she'd nap in an adjoining room.

John and Annie said good-bye and left. On the
drive home, Annie asked, "Will he ever walk again,
Dad?"

"We don't know, Annie. It's too soon to tell.
Probably not, though. We're hoping he can at least . . .
move . . . his arms." He felt awful saying that to a thirteen-year old. "More than likely, he'll never walk again.
He . . . he might not be able to move anything except
his head."

John began crying uncontrollably, the deep, painful weeping of a father for his son. He felt helpless to ease Ben's suffering or his own.

Annie shared his pain. Without shame, they cried together the entire trip home. When they reached the Hankinsons, John wiped his eyes and said, "I'm sorry, Annie. I couldn't help it."

"That's okay, Dad. I understand. You know what? I bet Ben makes a miracle happen. That's what I think."

"I hope you're right." He smiled at the simple innocence of a thirteen-year old. He hoped spending Christmas Eve with her and the Hankinson family would bring a modicum of joy into her day.

He thought he needed to hear laughter and to share in their friends' family gathering, but it didn't work. After an hour, he wished he were at the hospital with Ben and Nancy.

Finally, John thanked John and Bonnie for their kindness, left Annie with them, and drove the short distance to his own house. The family pets had to be fed, watered, and let outside. He watched twelve-year-old Winnie hobble down the steps. She didn't look good, and he wondered if she missed Ben.

When he finished, he looked around the empty house and saw Ben's hockey bag sitting by the back door. John reluctantly emptied the bag, holding up the torn jersey, breezers, and socks, and decided there was no point saving them, so he tossed them into the garbage. He took the rest of the gear upstairs, where he stood in the doorway and gazed into Ben's partially lit room.

He knew he shouldn't, but he couldn't help thinking, *He might never walk into this room again. How can something so tragic happen so fast? It's been like a runaway train since he was hit. Nothing could be done, and now . . .*

He slid down the door frame and landed on the floor with a thud. Winnie and Phoebe came to him, lying beside him and placing their heads in his lap. He was alone with his grief, but not entirely. As he cried, he thought of Ben.

I'd take a bullet for you, Benny. I'd cut off an arm or leg, or I'd give up an eye if I could change anything, but, after watching you lying there so helpless, knowing you might never move again, I . . . I don't . . . know . . . if I could trade places with you. I'm sorry for being so selfish.

He remained motionless with the dogs, gazing into the darkened room.

After a while, he stood and went into the den, looking for a clipping he saved. He dug through his files and found it after a few minutes, then he sat in an armchair and scanned the article.

When he found the passage he wanted, he read it aloud to the assembled animals. "A father doesn't raise heroes. He raises sons. If you treat them like sons, they'll turn out to be heroes, even if it's just in your own eyes."

You're my hero, Benny. You always will be, no matter what.

He put away the article, said good-bye to the dogs, turned out the lights, and locked the doors. The following day, Nancy's mother, sister, and husband would arrive from northwestern Minnesota to stay in the house with Annie and the animals. As he walked to his car, John wondered if life for them would ever be normal again.

When he returned to the hospital, he was amazed to find a parking spot near the front door. Perhaps that was because it was Christmas Eve, and everyone went home. The temperature was ten degrees above zero, and the only sound was his boots squeaking on the frozen, packed snow.

He shuddered, stopped, and looked up into the sky. Northern lights glowed in the west, and a meteor streaked across the blackness before it disappeared. Maybe that was a sign. Or maybe he was just grasping at straws.

He gritted his teeth, straightened his back, and walked inside to be with his son and wife.

Ben and his mother were watching TV when John arrived and walked to the bed to kiss Ben's forehead. "How ya doin', Boo?"

"I'm okay. Look at the note my friends left me. They put it on my bed when I was sleeping earlier. Mom didn't want to wake me."

John picked up the piece of paper and read it. "That sure was nice of them. Have you had a lot of visitors?"

"It's been nonstop since you left," Nancy said. "Whitney just left, and your parents called. This is the first time all night no one's been here. I'd like to lie down in the next room awhile. Is Annie okay?"

"She's fine. She'll stay with John and Bonnie tonight. Your sister will bring her over tomorrow."

Nancy kissed Ben and left the room.

"Dad, did you ever see the movie about Dennis Byrd?" Ben asked. "It was called, *Rise and Walk.*"

"I don't think so. What was it about?"

"He played for the New York Jets. He broke his neck, but he eventually learned to walk again. Mom thought it was a sign. What do you think?"

John was momentarily at a loss for words. He thought he'd seen a sign a moment ago. "Maybe you're right. I remember that movie now. No one ever thought he could walk again. He was a study in courage and strong faith. Keep believing, Ben." John was amazed at his son's spirit. "I'm proud of you." No matter what, Ben would remain Ben.

It was a long day for everyone. Ben fell asleep shortly after speaking with his dad. Nancy decided to go home for a while, so John settled into one of the room's two chairs and watched TV.

Christmas Eve gave way to Christmas. Ben slept peacefully as the day celebrating the birth of Christ arrived.

Chapter Five

The Plans I Have for You

A T THREE O'CLOCK CHRISTMAS morning, John awoke with a start and realized something was wrong. He heard noises coming from Ben's bed and raced to his side.

Ben was gagging on his own mucus. He couldn't breathe. His eyes were open, pleading for help. John pressed the call button and watched in horror as Ben struggled to take in oxygen. The look on his face was alarming. John, near panic, leaned against the back of a chair, holding onto its frame for support as the nurses reconnected the ventilator.

Ben was in trouble, and John was helpless to do anything but stay close and try to reassure him everything would be all right. He called Nancy and told her to return to the hospital. In their hearts, both feared the worst.

After Ben quieted and Nancy arrived, the nurses took them outside and explained what happened. Ben had to remain on the ventilator until he was strong enough to breathe on his own.

"How long?" John asked.

"There's no way to tell. Days . . . maybe longer."

They returned to Ben's side. He was intubated again and couldn't speak, and the lack of communication made him frustrated and angry. It was a setback, but they resolved to get through it together.

Again, they were reminded of the value of staying in the moment. It was all they could do.

CHRISTMAS PASSED WITH little change in Ben's condition. The stream of classmates, friends, and well-wishers continued. Even though visitors to his room were limited to a few at a time, Ben welcomed the break, because that helped him survive the long days.

John and Nancy established a routine whereby at least one of them was with Ben at all times. They took turns returning home for a shower and change of clothes. Two days after Christmas, John returned to work for a few hours, but he soon discovered he couldn't concentrate. He spent all his time on the phone, talking about Ben. Even though he appreciated people's concern, the situation wore him out.

The ventilator in Ben's mouth was removed occasionally, but most of the time, it remained in place. His condition was still critical. By midweek, Ben was accustomed to all the white coats visiting him. Because it was a teaching hospital, students, interns, and nurses came and went regularly.

Ben and his parents created a unique system of communication. Nancy held up an alphabet chart. When she pointed, Ben clicked his tongue against the roof of his mouth. With her help, he gathered his courage and asked a group of six doctors a very important question: "W . . . A . . . L . . . K?"

They understood, and the resident in charge said, "No, Ben. We don't think so. Too much time has passed. If some part of your body was going to move, it would've done so by now. I'm sorry."

The doctors left.

Nancy dropped the card and rushed to Ben's bed, expecting to find him in tears. Instead, he had a sly smile.

When he started clicking, Nancy got the chart, and he spelled, "W . . . R . . . O . . . N . . . G."

"Good for you, Ben!" His essence had always been that his spirit was more than what happened to him. She refused to let herself judge him tragically. Ben deserved better than that. At that moment, she was very proud of her son.

"What's this, Ben?" she asked, picking up a picture frame.

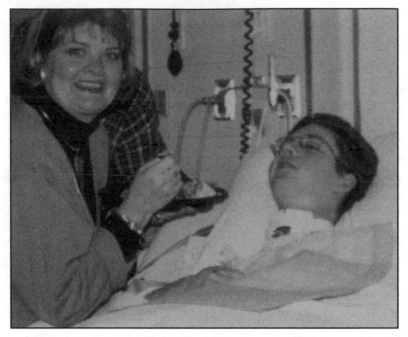

Nancy seldom left her son's side.

"R . . . E . . . A . . . D."

She read the Biblical quotation. "Jeremiah 29:11. 'For I know the plans I have for you, plans to give hope and a future.' Yes, Ben! God does have plans for you!" Tears filled her eyes.

Privately, Ben's doctor had told John and Nancy that the chances of Ben's moving again were slim. There had been too much bleeding and swelling. The damage was too extensive.

GRADUALLY, JOHN AND NANCY resigned themselves to the fact that their son would be a quadriplegic.

Their private conversations centered on the changes they had to make at home to accommodate their crippled son. That was reality. The hospital counselors encouraged them to begin preparing for long-term care for Ben at home. It wasn't easy, but, as each day passed without any sign of movement, they became more open about discussing their probable future.

"We'll have to remodel the house," John said.

"Yes," Nancy replied. "He won't be able to get to his room. We need to have someone look at converting the basement into an apartment."

It was a difficult, gut-wrenching decision.

As they concluded their conversation, Annie bounced in and said, "I have to go."

"Where are you going?" Nancy asked.

"Casey's picking me up. He's taking me to Mariucci Arena again to watch his hockey practice. Dad, will you come to my game later?"

"Yes, Honey. I'll be there." As difficult as it was for them to watch their daughter continue to play hockey with the boys' team, they felt it was important to support her and for one of them to attend her games. Nancy couldn't stand to watch anymore, so John usually went.

"Have fun, Honey," Nancy said.

"'Bye, Mom. 'Bye, Dad." Annie ran from the room and down the hall to meet her favorite college hockey player.

ON DECEMBER 27, BEN developed pneumonia. While his spirit remained intact, his body seemed to be withering and losing ground.

John and Nancy met Dr. Hertz, the pulmonary specialist, for the first time.

"Hi," he said. "My name is Marshall. I'm here for you and for your son."

The doctor's casual manner caught them by surprise. John and Nancy chatted with him for a while, and they learned that not only did Marshall have a son named Ben, he also had a daughter named Annie. John and Nancy felt the coincidence was significant.

"We're going to get this kid healthy," Dr. Hertz stated frankly. "Because of his injury, he can't clear his lungs, and he developed pneumonia. We'll treat him with antibiotics, and a respiratory therapist will work with Ben to help drain his lungs. We'll induce coughing by pounding on his chest, which is called lung therapy. We need to loosen the mucus so he can expel it."

He paused, then continued, "The frightening part is that the primary cause of death in quadriplegics is respiratory failure. That means we have to restore his health. I wouldn't tell that to Ben. He has enough to deal with as it is. Do you have any questions?"

John and Nancy were aghast. After all they'd been through, they suddenly had to face the possibility that Ben might die. They looked at each other in horror and fear.

Finally, Nancy found the strength to speak. "If the pneumonia progresses, what might we look for?"

"He'll have greater difficulty breathing, perhaps some pain and coughing. We'll see any change in his condition long before you do. I'll have our counselor stop by. She'll be very helpful."

He left them alone.

By then, Nancy and John had heard many times that due to the length of time since Ben's surgery, his lack of movement indicated lasting paralysis. The doctors spoke of Ben's condition as being permanent, and they seemed to expect John and Nancy to accept that and prepare accordingly. On some level they were doing precisely that.

"Nance, I haven't wanted to think about the worst in all this, because I didn't think I could deal with it," John admitted. "The other night, I started crying, thinking of all the things Ben and I used to do and probably never will do again." He paused, then pushed ahead. "As bad as it gets, any small sign of improvement, no matter how insignificant, will be terrific. That's all I've got to hang onto. Ben said the other day, 'Dad, I'm glad I have my faith.' It seems like you and Ben are strengthening mine."

"We're going through the grieving process," Nancy said, "longing for things that once were and wondering what the future holds. We'll eventually get past the grief and learn to deal with what's happening now. If we don't find peace and serenity in this, you know what the worst-case scenario is, don't you?"

"What?"

"We'll fall apart as a family. You and I will end up divorcing, and Annie will face problems in her life, while Ben's spirit will be as broken as his neck. Promise me, Honey, if you feel yourself slipping too far into the past or the future, you'll talk to me, okay? I . . . I promise to do the same for you." Her eyes were moist.

John realized they had reached a watershed moment in their lives. "I promise."

They held each other, allowing the love they felt for each other and their children to be rejuvenated by the commitment they would both honor.

BEN'S PNEUMONIA PERSISTED, and his condition worsened. On January 3, his left lung collapsed, and the Peytons' world felt like it collapsed with it. Not only was there no indication of voluntary movement from Ben's body below the neck, he was in serious danger of dying. The battle took a vicious, terrifying turn, and the doctors fought to keep the broken boy alive, but the pneumonia was persistent.

For the third time in ten days, Ben was prepped for emergency surgery. Dr. Hertz arrived and took John and Nancy aside.

"We're very concerned about his health," Dr. Hertz said. "His left lung collapsed because air became trapped in the pleural cavity between the lung and his chest wall, keeping his lung from filling with air. We have to inflate that lung, so we'll insert a small tube into his chest to evacuate the air around the lung. Then it can re-expand."

"What if it doesn't?" John asked, his voice shaking.

"The chances of his fighting off pneumonia with only one lung aren't good. I'm confident we can reinflate it, though. Once that's accomplished, we'll perform a tracheostomy, which will create an opening through his neck into his trachea. I'll insert a breathing tube directly into the trachea, which will breathe for him mechanically. Given Ben's physical condition, it's important to have both lungs operating at full capacity."

"How long will the tube have to stay in?" Nancy asked.

"The opening in his trachea will remain until he's out of danger. Unfortunately for Ben, the tube also prohibits speech by interrupting the flow of air to the voice box. He'll be angry and frustrated at not being able to communicate. I'll keep you informed as we move forward. Generally, an operation of this kind takes a couple hours."

As Dr. Hertz walked away, John said, "Now I'm really scared. I thought we were out of the woods, at least as far as . . ."

Nancy put her arms around her distraught husband and said, "I know. Do you know what Ben told me today?"

"What?" John stepped back and pulled out his handkerchief.

"'Mom, I just want to be happy and have a good life.'"

"What did you say?"

"I said, 'No problem, Ben. You'll be happy. You'll find a way.' He'll survive this, John, like everything else. He'll make the best of whatever he's got. He has God's gift of grace, and he won't let his body distract him."

Nancy was able to see events unfolding with amazing clarity and calm. "Once we survive this temporary setback, Ben's life will start over. He'll almost be reborn. God is with all of us. Ben's in His hands, and I'm okay with that. Are you?"

"Yes, I am." John said this with surety. He couldn't imagine going through such a thing without Nancy, and he thanked God for giving him a wife with undying faith.

AFTER THE OPERATION, Ben was wheeled into his room. He awoke some time later with a hole in his throat. The tracheal tube passed through an opening in his neck brace and connected to a ventilator. Before the pneumonia and collapsed lung, his spirits had been high and his outlook positive. The steady stream of friends, teammates, and visitors from the community kept him too busy to worry about his body.

Despite the doctor's negative comments about any bodily movement, Ben kept hoping that he would move again someday, even if that was just his shoulder. He hadn't given up. The most difficult part of his day were the long hours at night, when he was alone with his thoughts. Without the presence of others, he had to face his fears alone.

All he could do was internalize his thoughts. *Everybody has to deal with a problem in life. Mine came a little earlier than most. I was lucky to have seventeen years. Some people don't even get that much. I can still do anything I want. I have my mind. I haven't lost that.*

"Ben, do you want to try to tell me what you're thinking?" Nancy asked.

John returned to the room just then and overheard Nancy's question. "Benny? Want to click, then Mom and I can try to help you speak with us?"

"Y . . . E . . . S."

They spent the next hour acting out a primitive, comical game of charades. With the help of an alphabet chart and chalkboard, they slowly learned what was on Ben's mind.

"I don't think it can get any worse," he told them. "No point complaining. If paralyzed, okay. Is worse in my head than in reality."

John and Nancy had trouble focusing and were proud of their son.

"Yes, Ben," Nancy said. "We'll all learn to deal with it in our own way."

"I will be thankful for whatever I have." When Ben finished, he was worn out. After eating a few ice chips, he fell asleep.

JOHN AND NANCY DISCOVERED, just as Ben had, that the long, dark nights were the worst. During daylight, they had visitors to chat with, phone calls to make, and the clicking game to play with their son.

Once, Dr. Hertz said, "I never knew anyone had so many friends as you folks. Where do they all come from?"

Ben nodded.

"One of my friends told me," Nancy replied, "that the reason people come here is because they have to. They feel better for it." She smiled and looked at Ben.

"Makes sense," the doctor said. "Still, in all my years at this or any other hospital, I never saw so many people coming to visit just one patient. It's amazing."

"Yes, it's pretty neat, isn't it?" she asked.

A SHORT TIME LATER, Dr. Haines stopped by to speak with Ben and his parents. "I wanted to discuss some of the movement Ben's been experiencing. I want you to understand that the jerking he occasionally observes is reflexive. We call it spasticity. It's a sudden, involuntary contraction of muscle. The spasticity isn't dangerous, and, in time, we can control it with drugs. It's too soon for that now, however."

"How can you tell it's involuntary?" John asked.

"We test for it. Jerking like that is an inherent byproduct in this kind of injury. Ben's motor reflexes are gone, and his sensory reflexes are impaired, too. Those include the ability to sense hot and cold temperatures. Once he leaves the hospital, you'll have to be careful about exposing him to either extreme. He won't know when he's cold or hot."

"Ben's convinced that the jerks indicate some sort of stimulus to his legs," Nancy said.

"I wish I could tell you he's right, but I can't." He looked at Ben in sympathy.

Ben remained silent. *We'll see*, he thought.

"As we move forward, Ben will begin to experience problems controlling his bladder. He'll have to be catheterized twenty-four hours a day. There is a device called a baclofen pump that can be implanted under the skin. We can program the pump to release required dosages of certain drugs to help control your bladder, Ben. That's still off in the future, but I wanted you to know. Any other questions?"

"I guess not," John said. "Thank you, Doctor, for all you've done." He tried to accept whatever the future held, but that never came easily for him. Too much had changed.

After Dr. Haines left, Nancy asked, "Ben, what are you thinking?"

Ben was overwhelmed by his classmates support.

Ben began clicking, and Nancy wrote words on the chalkboard.

"He is wrong. I will move some."

Nancy spoke the words as her son clicked, fearing he was setting himself up for disappointment and misery, but she couldn't destroy his hopes. "If anyone can, Boo, it's you."

Chapter Six

And He Did

BEN'S DAYS AT UNIVERSITY HOSPITAL became routine and repetitive after the tracheostomy. The tube remained in his trachea, and he slowly grew accustomed to it. He regained some strength, and, with the help of the acute-care staff, doctors, and his parents, his health improved a little every day.

One night shortly after the tube was inserted, Ben woke gagging and choking. Something was wrong with his tracheal tube. It had become dislodged and wasn't functioning. The male nurse on duty came into the room after hearing the noise, took a quick look at the machine, and left.

Ben panicked. His eyes darted back and forth, and he clicked his tongue as loudly as he could.

No one responded. He couldn't feel any air entering his lungs and grew dizzy.

IN THE NEXT ROOM, something awoke Ben's father. He rubbed his eyes and looked at his watch, seeing it was three o'clock in the morning. He stood, stretched, and silently walked next door to look in on Ben.

Immediately, he saw something was wrong. Ben looked at him in terror, making John wonder if his son had a bad dream.

John rushed to his side and heard Ben clicking furiously. It was clear the boy was frightened. John looked at the tracheal tube and realized it had become detached from the opening in Ben's neck. He ran for a nurse.

He brought back the same nurse who'd been in the room earlier. He quickly replaced the tube, and Ben was able to breathe again. When John found out what happened, he became concerned. He confronted the nurse, who immediately defended himself and dismissed the incident.

John vowed that as long as Ben was attached to the tracheal tube, he'd never be left alone again.

The following day, John and Nancy spoke to the doctor about the nurse's behavior. All agreed it would be best if the nurse was assigned to another station. That proved to be the only negative experience Ben had with any of the staff at the hospital. He loved the people who cared for him, and he knew he was fortunate to be there.

The day after the incident with the nurse, January 6, Nancy walked into the room and saw Ben was excited about something. As she later told John, "It sounded like we had a cricket in the room."

She looked at him and saw excitement in his eyes and immediately worried that another incident had occurred. She moved quickly to his bed.

He was clicking rapidly and gesturing with his eyes. He wanted her to watch his right hand. He smiled and slowly spelled the word, "Watch."

Nancy stared at the inert hand. By then, his hand and fingers had atrophied and were hard for her to look at. She raised her head and looked into Ben's eyes, and he flicked his gaze back toward his hand.

She looked down and saw a slight, almost imperceptible twitch of his thumb. Startled, she stared intently. A moment later, his index finger moved a tiny bit.

"Oh, Ben! Really?" She looked up and saw his eyes twinkling with delight. He was smiling!

Although he moved them only a fraction of an inch at first, gradually, with effort, he could move both thumb and index finger. Nancy was thrilled.

"Can you do it again?" she asked cautiously.

Ben gestured with his eyes, and she watched as he once again moved his right index finger and thumb. Nancy wrapped her arms around him and said happily, "I have to call your dad."

Ben and his parents were ecstatic. Doctors arrived soon afterward and observed the slight movement, asking Ben to repeat it. The smiles on their collective faces said it all. They weren't seeing spasticity. Ben had consciously moved those digits.

I told you guys I'd move something, and I did, Ben thought happily.

That simple movement meant that someday he might be able to feed himself, dress himself, operate a wheelchair joystick, or even catheterize himself.

"If he can move his fingers, why not his shoulder and arm?" John asked Nancy when they were away from Ben, discussing the event. "You know, I feel selfish and wrong to think this, Nance, but, my God. What a relief! That means we won't have to feed him for the rest of our lives. If he can move his arm, he can take care of himself. Am I wrong to feel this way?"

"No. Ben predicted this. Who knows what else he can do? Let's not get too far ahead of ourselves. One little victory at a time."

THE FOLLOWING DAY, as the doctors made their rounds and stopped to observe Ben's thumb-and-finger action, Ben clicked a question. With Nancy's help, he asked, "Now what do you think? Will I ever walk?"

Ben's bright-blue eyes stared intently as he awaited the doctors' response.

Dr. Haines paused, then said carefully, "I don't think so, Ben, but I never thought you'd move your finger, either."

84

Nancy saw a female intern standing to one side with tears in her eyes as she watched Ben. It was a moving moment for everyone.

The staff left the room, and Ben smiled. Nancy saw pure joy in his eyes. She was so happy for him, she wanted to cry.

"Way to go, Ben!" she said.

ON JANUARY 12, a second prayer service was held on Ben's behalf at the Colonial Church in Edina. Once again, hundreds of friends, relatives, and neighbors attended. John, Nancy, and Annie were there, too. John's older brother, Jay, had returned from Colorado and spoke to the assembled group.

"When you pray for Ben," Jay said, "think of his spine as a piece of garden hose with a kink in it. Please imagine that same hose without a kink, with water flowing freely from one end to the other. That's what I'm praying for."

The vivid analogy was very moving. By the time Jay finished speaking, everyone in the audience felt convinced Ben would experience additional movement with God's help.

John spoke only briefly, mostly because the gathering was very emotional for him. "On Ben's behalf, thank all of you for your love and support. Nancy and I couldn't have gotten through this without you. You'll never know just how important you've been to Ben, or to Nancy, Annie, and me. Ben is getting stronger, his vitality and enthusiasm are high, and, as Brother Jay just said, with God's help, perhaps there are more miracles to come. From the bottom of our hearts, we thank you again."

THE DAY AFTER THE PRAYER SERVICE, January 13, Ben intentionally moved his right leg. Word spread quickly. His classmates heard later that day, and there was a mass exodus from Edina High. By midafternoon, the ICU unit was flooded with students.

School empties as word spreads.

Friends and relatives gathered that evening to watch Ben move his leg. As one, the happy visitors felt as if anything would be possible for Ben.

John and Nancy asked to see Dr. Haines.

"It's voluntary, isn't it?" John asked.

"Yes," Haines replied. "Everything indicates he's causing the leg to move."

"Why the right leg and not the left?" Nancy asked.

"Do you remember when I explained his initial injury? The C4 vertebra is higher up and was damaged on the left. C5, lower down, was damaged on the right."

"Will his left side ever show movement?" John asked.

"I doubt it, but Ben has already proved me wrong twice. Further improvement is up to him and the Lord."

LATE THAT NIGHT, after Ben fell into a deep, peaceful sleep, John stood beside his son's bed feeling emotional and excited about his future. "I promise you, Ben," he whispered, "someday, you'll swing a golf club again."

BEN GAINED STRENGTH as days passed. He had a new focus: The promise of additional movement and muscle coordination. With extreme effort, he spent hours laboring to flex his right hand and leg. Progress was agonizingly slow, but he had plenty of time and immense willpower. As he once told his mother, "I've got nothing but time, Mom."

The tracheal tube was removed on January 14. Unfortunately, Ben had to be slowly weaned off the breathing apparatus. At least he could talk again, and he was thrilled to be able to chat with people. He was happy not to click his tongue anymore.

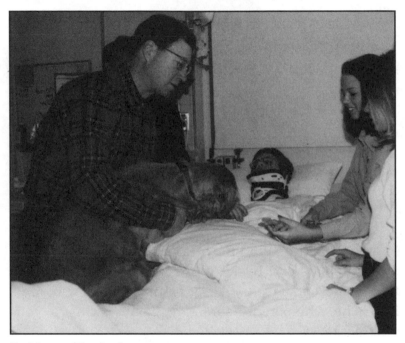

Dad brings Phoebe for a visit.

Ben's friends kept visiting him. Together, the young people laughed, joked, and talked about everything. Ben was also kept up to date on the success of the high-school hockey team. To everyone's pleasant surprise, the team kept beating superior teams it played.

The varsity coach stopped by one day and told Ben and his parents, "It's Ben's inspiration that's carrying the team."

"Really?" Ben asked.

"Yes. You know they dedicated this season to you, don't you?"

Ben felt honored and humbled. "No. I didn't know. That's really neat, isn't it, Dad?"

"It sure is, Ben. You've got a lot of good friends on that team, kids you grew up with."

"Those kids are hard workers," the coach said proudly. "Everyone's an overachiever."

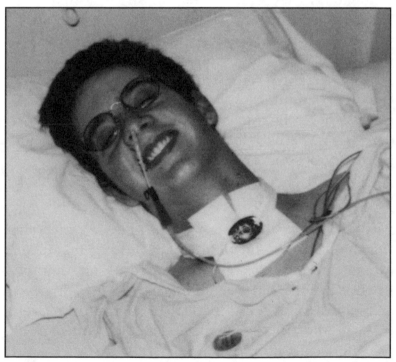

Always positive, always with a smile.

THE LOCAL MEDIA PICKED up Ben's story, and TV stations fit in an account of his accident and recovery into their periodic broadcasts. Articles about Ben were written in the *Minneapolis Star Tribune* and the *Saint Paul Pioneer Press*. The media covered Ben's story not just once but for months, retelling it many times.

John and Nancy were stunned at the way the Twin Cities responded so warmly to their son. Nancy thought she knew why.

"Everyone who comes into contact with Ben leaves feeling fulfilled somehow," she told John. "It's contagious. They want to help in any way they can. They want to support Ben. Through him, they leave with a sense of well being. I don't know if I've ever felt so grateful."

"You know, other than a few times when he couldn't communicate, Ben was seldom down," John said. "I never heard him whine or complain, and I don't think he ever felt sorry for himself. He's been incredibly positive and optimistic."

FINALLY, IT WAS ALMOST TIME for Ben to leave University Hospital. Nancy and John made arrangements for extensive, long-term, continuing care and therapy. Briefly, they considered taking him to a highly recommended spinal-cord institute in Denver, the Craig Institute, but Ben vetoed the idea. He wanted to be near his family and friends no matter what.

Without further discussion, they decided that the Sister Kenny Institute in Minneapolis would provide outstanding care and rehabilitation for Ben.

Toward the end of January, John and Nancy toured Sister Kenny and came away believing the facility was the right place for their son. Established in 1942 as a muscle rehabilitation center for polio victims, the institute became world renowned as a physical therapy center for patients with a variety of injuries and illnesses.

In 1997, Sister Kenny treated 108 patients with spinal-cord injuries. Affiliated with the Abbott Northwestern Hospital, the institute had a highly developed program for quadri- or paraplegics. The admissions counselor told John and Nancy that the staff would develop an individualized plan of care for Ben to regain as much independence as possible.

"You may not be aware that Elizabeth Kenny wasn't a nun," the counselor said. "She was an Army nurse who was unaware of conventional polio treatment in 1940, which immobilized limbs with splints. She used common sense and an understanding of anatomy to treat the illness's symptoms. She applied wet, hot packs to loosen muscles and enable limbs to be moved, stretched, and strengthened. She called this muscle reeducation. Thanks to Elizabeth, Sister Kenny Institute is now known for its progressive and innovative vision."

The counselor outlined the institute's spinal-cord injury program. In conclusion, she added, "Ben will receive state-of-the-art treatment."

Xsensor Pressure Mapping—sensor and computer technology that provides a cushion analysis for a patient's wheelchair seat, backrest, and mattress.

Biofeedback—a computer program that uses visual feedback to increase and strengthen function for weakened upper and lower extremities.

Functional Electrical Stimulation—a bike program that exercises the lower extremities.

Independence Square—a series of realistic environments that practice daily life situations, including car transfers, preparing a meal, shopping, dining out, and office work.

Bladder Management

Spasticity Management

Treatment to Decrease Loss of Bone Density

Education and Training on Adaptive Computer Controls—for people with limited or no hand function.

"Additionally, Ben will be part of a support group with other patients who are undergoing inpatient rehabilitation. Do you have any questions?"

"Yes," Nancy said. "Ben maybe has been a little spoiled by the University Hospital's acute-care staff. He's become accustomed to a certain amount of preferential treatment." She smiled.

The counselor smiled as well. "We've heard such things before, of course. The single most important thing we can do for your son is to allow him to regain his independence. Assuming there are no more medical issues to restrict his rehabilitation, Ben will be asked to work extremely hard twice a day."

"Hmmm. Sounds to me like you don't mollycoddle your patients or let them spend time feeling sorry for themselves."

The counselor laughed. "You said it better than I could, Mrs. Peyton. Ben needs to realize that if he hopes to care for himself, at whatever level that will be, it's completely up to him. We'll show him how, but he has to do the work."

After touring the facility, John and Nancy reported back to Ben. Their family discussion was somber and heart wrenching. Ben would become part of a program for patients with little or no hope of substantial recovery. The tenets of the program depressed him, and he vowed to prove the doctors wrong.

The rehabilitation program at Sister Kenny put everything into perspective for the family. John and Nancy resigned themselves to the fact that despite the slight movements Ben controlled, in the long term, he would undoubtedly be seriously handicapped. That was hard for the family to accept, but Ben's parents knew they had to move on and begin Ben's rehabilitation no matter what direction it took.

Chapter Seven

The Long Road Back

ON JANUARY 21, BEN tearfully said good-bye to the staff at University Hospital. An ambulance carried him to Sister Kenny Institute, where he began a long, difficult period of recovery. His first few days there were foreign and lonely. Adjusting from the personal care he received at University Hospital to the new environment wasn't easy.

The first time Ben was taken to physical therapy for treatment, Nancy watched in horror as the therapist placed Ben on a mat and worked his legs back and forth in what seemed a rough, uncaring manner.

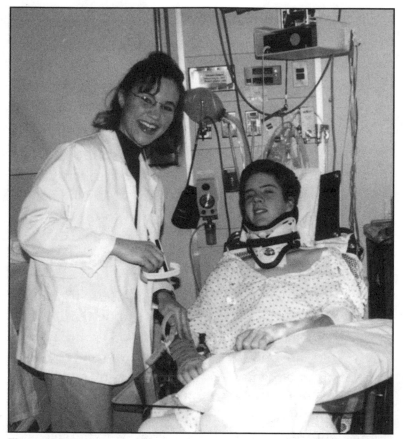

Time to move on.

Ben felt increasingly disoriented. Blood left his head, and he felt faint. "Mom? I don't feel too good. I'm dizzy."

"Are you sure he should sit up like that?" Nancy asked the therapist.

"Yes," she replied. "Don't worry. The dizziness is normal and will pass quickly. We need to put Ben in various positions as quickly as possible."

Progress was nonexistent at first. Ben had no sense of his body. He couldn't tell where his arms or legs were at any moment, and everything was confusing. The therapists worked his body through vigorous range-of-motion exercises. His twice-daily sessions were grueling. By the end of each one, Ben felt exhausted.

Unlike his stay at University Hospital, Ben had little time to spend with visitors. The workouts were long and lonely. More than once, he told his parents how different the staff was compared to the hospital.

"How do you mean, Ben?" Nancy asked.

"I kinda feel like I'm just a number here," Ben said. "It's not as personal as the university."

"They treat a lot of patients, Ben. If you remember, they warned us that it would be hard work."

"It's part of the program, Boo," John added. "They said no one gets babied around here. They have a job to do, which is to get you to a place where you can take care of yourself."

Nancy added, "Remember, all the work you're doing will help bring back whatever muscles or nerves you have that can still function," She said. "If you don't work every muscle, it'll atrophy and will never function."

FOR THE NEXT THREE WEEKS, no matter how hard Ben tried, nothing more moved except for his right shoulder and elbow in small ways. His left side remained completely paralyzed. It was important for him to keep up his overall strength. Pneumonia was still a concern, and one day, Ben's therapist told Nancy something very startling.

Nancy mentioned it to John later. "Ben needs fifty percent of his caloric intake just to breathe. The average person needs only two percent."

"You mean that half of the energy he expends every minute is just to breathe? No wonder he's so tired."

"Yes, and that's why his progress is so slow. We must be patient, and so must Ben."

"Yeah, but you heard him. He has no patience with all of this so far. He wants to see results—immediately."

GRADUALLY, THOUGH, BEN'S attitude toward the staff and treatment at Sister Kenny changed. *I don't have time to feel sorry for myself,* he thought. *This rehab business is just one more piece of the puzzle to a whole life.*

From then on, he resigned himself to working even harder on all phases of recovery. The physical and occupational therapy sessions often left him sweating and exhausted. He kept watching for small signs of improvement. Although the changes he felt taking place weren't readily apparent to others, he was convinced there were more exciting days ahead.

Encouraged, he maintained his sense of humor.

SOON AFTER BEN MOVED to Sister Kenny, John called Nancy.

"Hi, Honey," Nancy said. "How was Annie's game? Did they win?" Her face suddenly turned white, and the receiver slipped from her hand. She picked it up and slowly sat in a chair. "Oh, no. Not Annie."

Her team had made it to the regional playoffs for the state Pee-Wee-B Boy's Hockey Tournament. In the final period, an opposing player checked Annie hard against the boards.

"How bad is it?" Nancy asked. "Broken collar-bone? Good Lord. What next? How is she? Do you want me to come to the hospital? Okay. Call me if anything changes."

She hung up and stared at the blank TV screen. Slowly, she took a deep breath and tried to stay in the moment.

As if sensing the fresh agony in Nancy's voice, Winnie slowly rose and limped to Nancy's chair. She gently rested her whitened, aged muzzle on one knee and sighed.

Nancy laid her hand on the dog's head and stroked her soft hair. "Oh, Winnie, old girl. What's next?"

BEN'S THERAPY CONTINUED. The daily schedule was daunting. The doctor in charge of his care told his parents, "Ben will have to work harder than most Olympic athletes. The difference is, he won't be working for a medal."

"How's he doing?" Nancy asked.

"He's progressing. He never complains, and it seems that his frequent visitors help motivate him. We aren't accustomed to having cheerleaders present during therapy, but they all seem to have a good time."

John and Nancy looked at Ben's new schedule.

Early days at Sister Kenny.

7:00 A.M.	Occupational Therapy
8:30 A.M.	Physical Therapy
10:00 A.M.	Psychologist
12:00 P.M.	Lunch

"In the afternoon," the doctor said, "the entire routine is repeated."

"Wow," John said. "This goes on six days a week?"

"We're beginning the process of transfer. That means Ben will essentially be reborn. We'll take him back to the beginning of his learning curve—as an infant, if you will—but everything will be noticeably sped up."

"Can you be more specific?" John asked.

"I'm sorry. Ben has to relearn how to eat, dress,

wash, brush his teeth, and comb his hair, all with special tools. Eventually, he'll learn to catheterize himself."

"I hesitate to ask about that."

"That's the hardest of all. First, he has to inject the head of his penis with a needle to numb the tissue. Then he must insert a long tube through the opening to his bladder. Once it drains, he can remove it. If he's out in public, the tube can remain in place and drain into a bag he'll carry. It's not a pleasant image, but that's the reality."

"Good Lord," Nancy said.

THE NEXT TIME NANCY VISITED her son during one of his therapy sessions, she noticed his glasses kept slipping of his sweaty forehead. She didn't mention it, but she wished something could be done.

At one point, Ben looked up. His glasses were askew, perched at an angle on the end of his nose. He noticed her staring and laughed. "I know. I look like a nerd, don't I?"

Nancy giggled. "You do look silly. There must be a way to keep those glasses in place."

"If you figure it out, let me know."

LATER THAT NIGHT, NANCY mentioned the incident to John. The following day, John went in to have new glasses fitted, and the doctor asked how his son was doing.

"He's fine, Walt. Right now, though, he has trouble keeping his glasses on. We can't figure out how to adjust them to keep them from slipping down. You have any ideas?"

"We can fix that."

The following day, an ocular specialist visited Ben at Sister Kenny. In moments, he adjusted Ben's glasses so they no longer slid down his nose.

When Nancy heard about it, she said, "Somehow, good things just keep happening to us." More gratitude.

DURING FEBRUARY, THE LOCAL MEDIA continued covering Ben's story. Television stations reported on his condition with surprising regularity. One of the more-popular morning radio shows even elected to broadcast their program from Ben's room. With Ben's parents' permission, of course, and with John present, the show was broadcast at seven o'clock one morning.

Once they were on the air, the host asked Ben, "What's the hardest part of all this for you?"

"I guess it was early on, when I realized my life would never be the same."

"What's been the most surprising?"

"That's easy. It's the overwhelming support I've received from so many people. I expected friends and relatives to be there for me, but so many other people have been very supportive and encouraging, too, like you. I'm very grateful."

"You seem to be a very upbeat, positive young man. However, at some point you must've felt sorry for yourself, right?"

"I actually didn't feel too bad, because even in my physical state, I was better off than a lot of others, like kids in Third World countries or those born with multiple sclerosis. I could've been totally paralyzed, but I wasn't. Other people have degenerative illnesses and won't ever get better.

"In my case, the bad stuff's behind me. I'll either stay the same or improve. I kept thinking that the only person who has the greater right to bitch and whine is the person who's worse off than everyone else. I wasn't even the most seriously injured patient in ICU when I was there."

"What about the future?"

"You know, I've tried not to think too far ahead, but it's hard not to. I know things will be different, but I haven't given up yet. I still think I can walk someday, and that's been my main focus lately. If not? Well, I still have my mind. Maybe I'll be a radio talk-show host."

The host laughed. "Anything else you'd like to say before closing?"

"I used to be a pretty good golfer. Someday, I'd like to play to my handicap."

The host laughed again. "Good for you, Ben, and nice pun, too. You're a study in courage, young man, and an inspiration for us all. Good luck. Let's do this again if you're willing."

"Sure. You bet. Any time," Ben said enthusiastically.

On February 26, John received a phone call from a friend in the golf business.

"John? Bruce McIntosh. How's Ben doing?"

"Hi, Mac. He's fine. How are you?"

"Good, thanks. Say, have you heard of the golf show we're putting on at the Metrodome?"

"Yeah, I have. I didn't know you were involved in it, though."

"Somehow, I got roped in. Anyway, I have tickets for you and Ben. It's next Saturday."

John wondered if Ben wanted to go. It might be too depressing for him. "I don't know, Mac. Ben hasn't been out of the hospital yet, you know. I'll have to see if he's interested."

"I understand. The reason I thought you'd like to bring him is that part of the show features a guy who is also paralyzed but still manages to play golf. He can hit a drive over 260 yards! It might be fun for Ben to watch him."

"Really? That might be a good thing for him to see. I'll let you know, Mac. Thanks."

"My pleasure. If you decide to come, I'll arrange it so you can pull into the player's ramp and park inside. Just let me know."

Ben was due for his first outing away from Sister Kenny, and John and Nancy thought the golf show would be a perfect first trip for him. John invited his friend, Boomer. With Annie, they made plans for the day.

John borrowed a handicapped-accessible van, and they picked up Ben from Sister Kenny. John saw

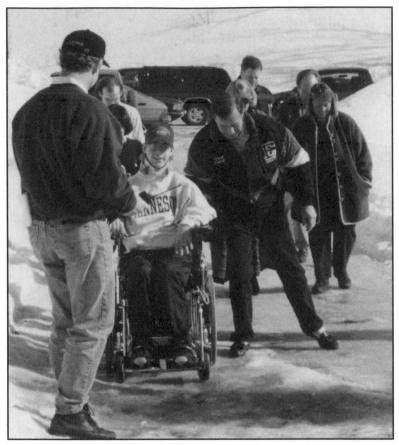

A welcome, first outing.

Ben was excited but apprehensive, too. They drove the short distance to the Metrodome, parked inside, and opened the van's side door.

Bruce met them and shook hands. John engaged the hydraulic lift, and Ben was wheeled onto the concrete. They followed Bruce inside and onto the playing field.

Dennis Walters, the handicapped golfer, was just beginning his show. He sat on a specially made swivel seat attached to a golf cart. A microphone ran from his ear down to his mouth so he could talk to the crowd.

"In 1973, after graduating from North Texas State," Dennis began, "I was busy working on my golf game. My dream was to become a professional golfer, and I planned to enter Qualifying School the following fall.

"Shortly before Q School, I fell off a golf cart and injured my spine. Ultimately, I became a T-12-level paraplegic and was told I'd never walk again. That made playing golf highly unlikely."

Dennis paused, swiveled the chair, positioned his legs, and whacked the golf ball on the tee before him. It traveled straight out and up, its flight finally halted by a net strung across the stands in center field.

"After five months of rehabilitation, I went home. With my father's help, we built a swivel seat to mount on a golf cart." He stopped and hit another ball just as hard as the first.

"Now I can get around the golf course and swing a club about as well as the next guy." He hit another ball.

"My point is, if there's something you really want to do, no matter how impossible it seems, with enough hard work and perseverance, you can do it!" He hit a fourth ball as Mac approached and whispered quickly in his ear.

"I'm told there's a young man here today recovering from an injury similar to mine," Dennis said. "Ben Peyton was injured playing hockey last December. Come on out here, Ben!"

John wheeled Ben to meet Dennis. Ben felt embarrassed by the attention, but he was fascinated by what the older man had accomplished.

"You're a golfer, Ben?" Dennis asked.

Mac held a microphone to Ben's lips. "Yes, I was," he said quietly.

"Do you miss it?"

"I haven't had much time to miss it yet, but I'm sure I will this summer."

"Tell you what, young man. If you set your mind to it, you'll find a way to swing a golf club again. I promise. Good luck, son. How about a nice round of applause for young Ben?"

The audience gave Ben a thundering ovation. By then, most people in town knew Ben's story. Their applause showed they wished him well. Ben and John were moved by the wonderful show of support.

Dennis spent the next thirty minutes demonstrating how truly skilled he had become, hitting

A humble seventeen-year old responds to the audience.

106

golf balls with every club in his bag, while Ben watched closely.

When it was over, Ben, feeling impressed, told John, "That was really cool, Dad. I didn't think I wanted to come, but I'm glad I did."

John recalled his private promise to his son and thought that what they'd just witnessed was amazing. He turned to Mac. "Thanks a million, Mac. That meant a lot to Ben and me."

"You're welcome, John. I have to go upstairs now. Take Ben around to some of the booths and get him something to eat. I'll see you later. Take care, Ben."

"Huh? Oh, thanks, Mr. McIntosh."

Ben's hockey coach was at the show, too. He joined them and spent the next ninety minutes visiting vendors while Ben ate everything he could.

"Anything else you'd like, Benny?" the coach asked.

Ben looked at him slyly and said, "Yeah. A beer." His eyes twinkled.

The coach nudged Boomer and asked, "What do you think?"

"Better clear it with his old man first."

They looked at John, who shrugged.

"Do you have a preference?" the coach asked Ben.

"Budweiser."

"You got it. Be right back."

Ben polished off the Bud and held the empty cup out to Boomer. "Just one more, okay, Benny?"

He brought Ben a second cup and before long they were all giggling and laughing, because Ben was getting tipsy.

"Don't say anything to Mom, okay, Annie?" Ben asked. "Promise?"

"About what?" She was just glad to see Ben having so much fun.

After Ben finished his second glass of beer, John said, "Ben, we'd better check that bag."

"Oh, geez. I forgot." He was catheterized and carried a bag under his coat.

John wheeled him to the rest room and emptied the bag. They returned to the floor of the dome, and Ben promptly asked for an ice cream cone. He was able to grasp objects by then, although with difficulty, and he managed to bring his right arm to his face. It wasn't yet a smooth motion, but it was still miraculous.

Unfortunately, the beer impaired Ben's already shaky motor skills. All four watched him raise the cone to his mouth, then, in one quick move, jam the mound of chocolate chip ice cream into his right eye.

The ice cream fell loose and into his lap. John, Annie, Boomer, and the coach waited for Ben's reaction. When he laughed, they joined him. He insisted on eating the ice cream, anyway. With Annie's help, he finally consumed it all.

By the time they brought Ben back to the institute, he wasn't feeling well. His system wasn't used to the variety of foods he had consumed. "I'm sicker than a dog, Dad. Better hurry, or I'll woof all over the van."

They got him back to his room just in time. Everything he ate that day came back up. Once he emptied his stomach, he felt better. He had no regrets, though. For a first outing from the hospital, it was a blast. He'd had a wonderful time, and, in the back of his mind, he had the image of Dennis Walters hitting golf balls from his swivel seat.

Why not? Ben wondered. *If I could just get some more movement in my arms.* . . . He fell asleep with that thought.

Chapter Eight

He Will Always Be Ben

S HORTLY AFTER THE GOLF SHOW, John and Nancy agreed to do another in-depth interview with a local TV station.

"Ben's story has touched the entire Twin Cities," the reporter said. "We wanted to find out not only how he's been progressing, but how John and Nancy Peyton have managed to cope with such a tragic accident. First of all, how's Ben doing?"

John looked at Nancy, who nodded for him to speak. "He's doing great. He's at Sister Kenny undergoing rehabilitation. He's able to move his right shoulder, arm, hand,

and fingers, as well as his right leg. Thus far, the left side of his body hasn't shown any sign of recovery, but we're hopeful."

"When the accident first happened, how'd you cope?"

"We were in shock, of course," Nancy said. "Until the doctors diagnosed Ben's injury, we thought it was only temporary. As each moment passed, however, the prognosis became bleaker. At first, our fear was total. John and I discussed what paralysis meant and decided that we couldn't project into the future. We knew God was with us. With our faith and His grace, everything was possible.

"We realized early on that no matter what the outcome was, Ben would always be Ben. As long as he had his mind, spirit, and energy, we'd have him."

A very proud mother.

"Yes, but wasn't his life in danger at one point?"

"That was probably the low point," John said. "All we could do was accept the fact that Ben was in God's hands. I remember thinking that once we got through the pneumonia and collapsed lung, it couldn't get any worse. Any improvement from then on was a big plus."

"We were terrified," Nancy said, "but we never lost faith that something remarkable would evolve from Ben's situation. We never tried to get too far ahead of ourselves or dwell on the bad things that might happen. You know all the various anonymous groups that talk about taking life one day at a time? Some of the time, that even was too long. We felt we needed to take that concept down to the hour and minute. We tried to stay in the moment."

"It seems pretty simple, and it's good advice for anyone. Anything else?" the reporter asked.

"Yes. We're extremely grateful to all the people who prayed for Ben and saw him during those early days. The support Ben received from the community was overwhelming."

"Thank you for your time. We all wish Ben continued good fortune and appreciate your sharing your thoughts with us."

Once the interview ended, the reporter told them, "It's amazing that Ben's story continues to capture people's attention."

"Why?" Nancy asked.

"Normally, human-interest stories get a lot of play, then are forgotten. By the following week, you're fortunate to see a sidebar on page three of the Metro section."

"What makes Ben's story different?" John asked.

"The fact that he injured himself playing hockey, for one. This town is nuts about hockey. Beyond that, he's a really neat kid. Every video I've seen of him shows him to be upbeat, personable, and full of energy. You should be very proud."

"Thank you. We are," Nancy replied.

ON THE LAST DAY OF FEBRUARY, Annie got off the school bus and ran up the walk to the front door of her house. Her arm was still in a sling from her broken collarbone. With difficulty, she opened the outer door with the same hand that held her book bag.

Then the door swung open unexpectedly, and she looked up at her mother. Annie felt a wave of concern immediately. "Mom? What happened?"

Nancy's eyes filled with tears. She knelt, set her daughter's book bag on the floor, and said, "Annie, I'm so sorry. Winnie died this morning."

"Oh, no! Not Winnie!" She threw her good arm around Nancy's neck and sobbed.

Mother and daughter shared tears and sorrow in the front hall of a house that had already seen its share of pain and suffering. After a while, they stood and walked into the kitchen.

"How'd she die, Mom?"

"Her heart just gave out, Sweetheart. Winnie was old."

Annie thought for a moment. "I bet I know why she died."

"Why?"

Annie said, "She died of a broken heart. Ever since her boyfriend, Sam, died last fall, she was never the same. Then, with Ben gone, it was too much for her."

"You might be right, Annie."

"Remember when Winnie and Sam got married and had a litter of puppies? Ever since then, I could always get her excited by saying, 'Where's Sam, Winnie?' She smiled, wagged her tail, and spun like a top. She and Sam were hunting buddies. This is so sad."

"I know. At least they're together now. I'll bet they're having a great time together. What do you think?"

"I'll bet you're right. I hope so, anyway."

DURING MARCH, BEN CONTINUED his therapy at Sister Kenny. Gaining strength every day, he worked hard to regain muscle tone and flexibility. He watched carefully for every new sign of improvement. His vitality and optimism remained high. Despite the doctors' words of caution, he was convinced he could bring his crippled body back to life.

John was present one day when Ben was connected to the biofeedback machine. He watched a moment. "Can you explain what's happening?" John asked.

"Of course," the therapist replied. "Ben's working with different muscle groups. It looks as if there's nothing happening, but we can see on the screen when a certain muscle is active. Let me show you." She waved him closer.

He peered at the screen. Ben was sweating profusely and breathing hard.

"What am I looking for?" John asked.

"Ben's working for blips. Every time a tiny blip appears on the screen, that's a win. It means there's muscle activity—a good sign. The blips are our only indication that he's working hard enough to create a positive response."

"One blip at a time, eh, Benny?" John asked.

Ben was panting. Between breaths, he said, "When we first started, it seemed hopeless, but each day we find a new blip, and that's encouraging."

John smiled and shook his head, feeling very proud of his son.

DURING THE WEEK OF MARCH 7, the Edina Hockey team moved through the playoffs for the Minnesota State Boys' Hockey Tournament. With his parents' help, Ben attended every game. The team kept winning, even though most observers felt they weren't the strongest team in the tournament.

On Saturday night, March 13, Edina played in the state championship game. The team had long ago dedicated the season to their friend, and, that night, they won the state tournament. No one had given them a chance, just as very few gave Ben one.

The overachieving hockey player, supposedly crippled for life, proved to be the inspiration his friends needed to succeed. At the end of the game, before the trophy presentation, Annie wheeled Ben onto the ice to celebrate with his friends. John and Nancy watched with pride as Ben circled the ice. Hundreds of thousands of people around the state watched on TV as the young man from Edina smiled, cheered, and cried at his team's victory celebration.

Edina High School—State Champs!

Television announcers watched Ben participate in the celebration on the ice. At the end of the broadcast, one announcer said, "What a fitting end to Edina's hockey season."

Personal video cameras captured the moving scene at center ice. John was barely able to hold his camera steady as he recorded the moment. Ben and his parents would always remember the feelings shared with friends and neighbors that night.

ON MARCH 26, IT WAS TIME for Ben to leave Sister Kenny. The staff had done all they could for him and would continue working with him as an outpatient for another nine months. Ben worked diligently to strengthen his crippled frame, never losing sight of his objective, and he dreamed of the day when he would walk again.

Ben had one last session with his physical therapist that day. Nancy stayed to drive Ben home when he finished. As she watched her son go through his routine, she noticed he seemed particularly driven to achieve a goal he'd set for himself. He sweated and groaned with every movement.

She stood transfixed as the therapist, who was attuned to Ben's mission, led him to the parallel bars. *What's he doing?* Nancy wondered.

The therapist stood behind Ben as he tried to support himself between the cold, metal tubes. Most of his weight seemed to be on his right side.

Last days at Sister Kenny.

Ben looked over his shoulder at the therapist, nodded, and looked at his mother. As he once did before, he gestured with his eyes and clicked his tongue like a cricket, but this time, he spoke the letters. "W . . . A . . . T . . . C . . . H."

Nancy's hand flew to her mouth as she watched her once totally paralyzed son. *Oh, Ben! Thank You, God! Thank You! Thank You!*

Three months from the day that Ben had last willfully moved either of his legs, aided by his therapist, Ben took his first step.

Ben was on his way—and he wasn't afraid.

Epilogue

THE FOLLOWING SUMMER, a golf tournament was held at the Braemar golf course. One hundred forty players paid one hundred dollars each to participate. Combined with a silent auction, thousands of dollars were raised for the Ben Peyton Foundation. Throughout the next two years, the money would be donated to patients suffering spinal injuries.

Ben continued receiving treatment at Sister Kenny throughout 1997 as an outpatient. According to the doctors, his progress was miraculous. Not only did he regain strength and movement in his right leg, but the left leg

Uncle Whit at the Edina Hockey Benefit.

began responding to treatment, too. Before he returned to school, Ben went to the institute to take—and pass—his driving test.

"We don't see too many C4-5s passing this test," the instructor said. "Congratulations!"

On the first day of school that fall, Ben walked unassisted up the sidewalk, the short flight of stairs, and through the front door to begin his senior year.

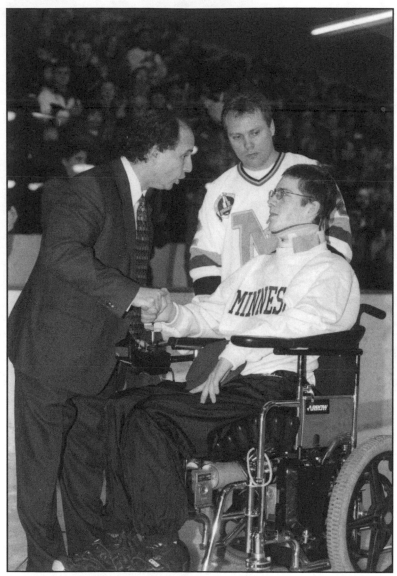

Senator Paul Wellstone, Curt Giles, and a grateful Ben Peyton.

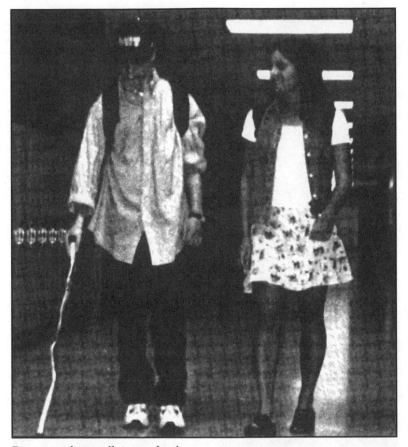

Ben vowed to walk into school.

He was chosen homecoming king in October. He wanted to walk unaided across the football field for the coronation, and he did. Ben graduated from Edina High the following year with his classmates.

He enrolled at the University of St. Thomas in the fall and moved into a dorm room with another freshman.

A popular choice as Homecoming King.

Ben became a much-sought-after public speaker in the Twin Cities for several years after he left Sister Kenny. His inspirational talks were sprinkled with humor. He spoke of the remarkable courage of many others he met at the institute, and, in particular, two friends who were very important to him.

Brian had a brain tumor and was paralyzed from the neck down. "He was a positive guy," Ben said, "faith oriented, with a family he cared deeply for. His daughter was deaf. Brian unselfishly moved his family from Bemidji to Fairbault, 250 miles, so his daughter could attend a school for the deaf. He was a man who never complained, who never said life dealt him a bad hand.

"Another friend of mine was Pat Patterson, a diabetic and double amputee. He loved hockey, had a wonderful sense of humor, and spoke in typical Minnesota Speak. We spent many hours listening to Garrison Keillor together."

Ben paused to collect himself. "Pat died this fall. I . . . I thought . . . he was one of the most courageous people I ever met. I'll miss him.

"I had my dark moments, too, but I always tried to keep a smile on my face for those who visited me. If they made the effort to come all that way in crappy winter weather just to see me, the least I could do was help them feel good about it.

"A good friend of my dad came in one day early on and gave me one of his AA sobriety medals. It sat on my nightstand for a long time until I finally moved my right arm. Once I saw what it had written on it, it put everything in perspective. The medal has the serenity prayer on it, which reads, 'God grant me the serenity to accept those things I cannot change, the courage to change the things I can, and the wisdom to know the difference.' I always thought that was a great message for anyone."

Ben typically concluded his talks with a question-answer period, and the questions were fairly predictable.

"How did you keep from feeling depressed?"

"I kept thinking that I had a good life. I'd been happy to play hockey and golf and spent time with my dad. As long as I could think and speak, well, I'd make the most of what I had. It could've been worse. I could've been killed or injured in a country where there was no care. In that regard, I was very lucky."

Mother and son—more than friends!

"How did your parents handle everything?"

"They were great. Mom, Dad, and my sister, Annie, were always there, sometimes all day. Mom's very spiritual, and, because of her faith, we all came to believe that even as bad as things were, God was with us. Somehow, she created a sense of calm that affected us all. I know they were very frightened, especially in the beginning, but I never saw much of it.

"We laughed and joked a lot. Here's one example. After I came home, Mom and Dad tried to unload me from the car into my wheelchair. Mom held the door, while Dad dragged me out. It wasn't going too well. He started mumbling and cussing because he couldn't quite get me into the chair.

"Mom watched and didn't say anything. Finally, I look down and said, 'Dad, you're standing on my foot!' We got quite a few chuckles out of that. My dad isn't the handiest guy in the world.

"There was another time at University Hospital when I had an accident with my bowels. The nurses were there, and so was Mom. Despite all the help, Dad rolled up his sleeves and cleaned me by himself. By the time he was finished, we were laughing like crazy at the whole thing.

"My dad's in the audience today. I was saving this for him for Father's Day, but I think I'll give it to him now. I hope I can get through it.

"Dad, I never realized how much a father could love his child . . ." He stopped when his voice broke. ". . . until . . . I was injured." Tears filled his eyes as he looked for his father.

Ben always concluded his talks by saying, "I'm very fortunate. Really. I'm the same person I was before the accident, but I know I'm different, too, if that makes any sense. I was given the opportunity to start over, to relearn everything again. Now, I can't rely just on my body. I have to use my mind much more than before.

"Thank you all for coming."

In 1998, Ben gave his last talk before an audience. When asked why he was quitting, he replied, "Because I don't want to be remembered as Ben Peyton the injured hockey player. My injury doesn't define my life. I'm not a saint. I'm just Ben."

ON JULY 23, 1998, JOHN fulfilled the promise he made to Ben when his son swung a golf club for the first time since his accident. He could hold it only with his right hand, but he hit the ball solidly. That was a wonderful moment for father and son.

BEN WALKS WITH A CANE TODAY. He wears a brace on his left leg and walks with a limp because that leg never fully recovered. His left arm doesn't have much strength or range of motion, but he continues to exercise, and he hopes that someday his weak arm and leg will strengthen. He has complete freedom of movement, mobility and independence in all other respects, and he lives in an apartment with a close friend.

A promise kept.

Freshman year, University of St. Thomas.

Ben graduated from St. Thomas on January 31, 2003, with a B.A. degree in economics and math. He's not sure what he wants for a career and is considering accounting or actuarial work. He also has an abiding interest in working for a charitable foundation, especially one devoted to helping spinal cord injury patients.

Everyone has a story to tell.
This is mine, I guess.
                    Ben Peyton

1995 Minnesota Sportsman of the Year presented by Ben's good friend, Curt Giles.

The Peytons.